JOAN CAMPBELL began taking in 'nighters' as ̠̠̠̠̠ more than a means of adding to the family income ̠̠̠̠̠̠ ̠̠̠ ears in the business, she and her husband Hugh r̠̠̠ ̠̠̠̠̠ ̠. In the same year Joan was awarded the coveted ̠̠̠̠̠̠ er Thistle for her outstanding contribution to to̠̠ ̠̠̠̠ ̠ntinues to write her monthly column, 'Tourism ' ̠̠̠̠̠̠ ̠blished in *The Northern Times*, and occasionally c̠̠ ̠̠̠̠̠̠ articles when time permits. She sits on the Highlands & I̠̠̠nds Tourism Awards board and represents Sutherland and Caithness for the Federation of Small Businesses. Joan is also assisting North Highland College to design a BA Degree in Tourism and Hospitality Management for the University of the Highlands & Islands and its partner colleges. Joan and Hugh are soon to move to their new home on the hill nearby, where Joan will continue to write.

Heads on Pillows

Behind the scenes at a Highland B&B

JOAN CAMPBELL

Luath Press Limited

EDINBURGH

www.luath.co.uk

First published 2009

ISBN: 978-1-906307-71-4

The paper used in this book is recyclable. It is made
from low chlorine pulps produced in a low energy, low emission
manner from renewable forests.

Printed and bound by The Charlesworth Group, Wakefield

Typeset in 11.5 point Sabon
by 3btype.com

The author's right to be identified as author of this book under the
Copyright, Designs and Patents Act 1988 has been asserted.

© Joan Campbell 2009

Contents

Acknowledgements		7
Foreword		9
Introduction		11
CHAPTER 1	A Busy Little Bee	15
CHAPTER 2	Over My Dead Body	21
CHAPTER 3	Heads on Pillows	29
CHAPTER 4	Going into Season	35
CHAPTER 5	John Dear and the Rabbit	43
CHAPTER 6	The Year of the Sheep	53
CHAPTER 7	Bums in Beds	77
CHAPTER 8	A Room with a View	83
CHAPTER 9	Taken Out by the SAS	93
CHAPTER 10	Entertaining the Mothans	103
CHAPTER 11	New Tricks for the Old Dog	113
CHAPTER 12	Tooth and Nail	119
CHAPTER 13	Gilding the Lily	133
CHAPTER 14	One for the Pot	157
CHAPTER 15	High Jinks and Hard Work	175
Conclusion:	What Will Tomorrow Bring!	175
Recipes to Ponder from the Kitchen of The Sheiling		181
Notes		185

Acknowledgements

THIS BOOK GIVES ME the opportunity to thank a long list of people, longer than I realised when I look back and think how much I owe to friends and family who helped keep the ship afloat, those who worked with me during the busy years, and those who came to the rescue when playing with horses or performing on stage lured me from the coal face: the late, very much missed, Barbara Jappy; Diane Mackay; Connie Mackay; Rina MacLeod; Cathy MacIntosh; Hazel Murray; Heather Simpson; Sandra Munro; Barbara Campbell; Debbie Murray and Katrina Geddes; but most of all for the man Himself, my own special Skimbleshanks, always behind me, ready to remind me, that never, not on his watch anyway, would anything ever be allowed to go wrong!

Joan Campbell

Foreword

THE TOURISM INDUSTRY is perhaps the most competitive industry in the world. In an age when potential visitors can visit the Arctic and Antarctica, not to mention everywhere in between, Scotland is competing with more than 200 comparable destinations across the globe. Many of these destinations offer a product which is very similar to what we have on offer here and they are competing for the same visitors we are. So what is there that Scotland can offer to stand out from the crowd? For me the answer is simple: our people.

Scotland is renowned the world over as a friendly country, where visitors can be assured of a warm welcome. Never before has the warmth of that welcome been as important as it is today. Globalisation makes differentiation increasingly difficult. However, the people are what makes a country, an industry, an individual business. It is the people who make that difference. And for the Scottish tourism industry, it is the people, individuals like Joan Campbell, who have made Scotland the success it is today – a must-visit, but more importantly, a must-return destination.

Joan has worked tirelessly during her many years in the industry, welcoming thousands of visitors from around the world to Scotland and ensuring that they have a truly memorable stay. Her commitment to quality, from the locally-sourced ingredients in her famous Scottish breakfast to her annual decorating sprees, has won her a string of awards including the ultimate tourism accolade – the Silver Thistle – and has kept visitors coming back year after year for more.

It's the enthusiasm and dedication of people like Joan that will help us ensure that Scotland fulfils its aspirations and more. Today's visitors are increasingly discerning and demand higher levels of quality all the time. But it's not simply the quality of the product that's important. In fact, that's the easy part. It's the quality of the service that can really make or break the visitor's experience. The customer is always right. The customer is king. These might sound like truisms but the simple fact is that making our customers happy is what tourism is all about. I hope that everyone involved in tourism will follow Joan's example and go that extra step to make their visitors' experience so memorable that they not only come back again but spread the word.

On behalf of VisitScotland, I would like to thank Joan for her many years of dedication to Scotland's most important industry. Her insight into what it's like at the coal face will prove an entertaining read and, I'm sure, will provide a few surprises along the way. I also hope it might encourage others to enter the industry. After all, as you will soon learn, not only is tourism Scotland's most important industry, it's also our most fun and exciting one.

Peter Lederer CBE
Chairman, VisitScotland

Introduction

BED AND BREAKFAST is an occupation dependent for its very survival upon the ability to keep everyone not just happy, but in holiday mood. And if those expectations are not met, the customer is right there, on hand, to let you know exactly how they feel about it!

We all know how things can go disastrously wrong when friends and family elect to stay together to celebrate occasions heralded as high-days and holidays. That being the case, can you imagine the scope for disaster when a variety of strangers get together with your family under one average-sized roof, everyone expecting everything to be absolutely perfect? And remember, it's up to you to see everyone keeps on smiling throughout their stay. Frightening, isn't it?

Well, it can be. It can also have unimaginable rewards, and with truth being more fascinating than fiction, now feels the right time to let you into some of the secrets lying behind the perfect image of a top-rated B&B.

Forty years ago, doing bed and breakfast was simply the acceptable way for many a homebound wife and mother to earn a bit on the side, to add to the family income, or to make some pin money. I thought that too – until I saw the potential. In driving bed and breakfast forward as a serious concern, I have found myself in some rather hair-raising situations. One day I went from cleaning the loos in the morning to meeting the Prince of Wales in the afternoon, my main concern on that occasion being to ensure the loose cap on my front tooth remained firmly in place, rather than flying into his fruit drink.

In time, the evening dresses of past cruising holidays were dusted down and given an airing at many glamorous occasions, all associated with tourism. This culminated in the night an ancient old dress seemed OK to wear to the prestigious Silver Thistle Award ceremony, attended by close on a thousand of the great and the good from within the industry. After all, I was up for no awards and my intention was to have a whale of a time – in the background. The shock on my face when presented the accolade of the year, VisitScotland's top Thistle Award for outstanding services to the tourism industry, is testament to the fact I was hoodwinked into believing I had only been invited in honour of my impending retirement from VisitScotland's Quality and Services Overseeing Committee, which I had served on for years.

I tell you this so you know that no matter the difficulties you face in achieving the best for the visitors taken into your home, you can reach for any star you keep within your sights. Mine was to give my paying guests the highest standards of comfort and hospitality and to help colleagues along the way. The route was peppered with many heartbreaking moments and much hilarity, as well as opportunities to be in places and meet people I would never have imagined. Take, for instance, today.

Engrossed in puzzling over finances as we set our sights on selling our B&B, The Sheiling, and building a new home, just as new-build costs were hitting the ceiling and selling houses taking a serious nosedive, an envelope with an ER Buckingham Palace stamp plopped through the letter box. It read:

The Master of the Household has received
Her Majesty's command to invite
Mrs Joan Campbell
to a Reception to be given at Buckingham Palace
by The Queen and The Duke of Edinburgh
(PS Do make an appointment with your dentist before then.)

I ask you, whatever next! Not too bad for a wee B&B wifie!

I

A Busy Little Bee

'Yes, I am. Really busy.' Trying to cover my impatience with a smile, foot poised for the off, I made the mistake of pausing that fraction of a second too long. The question came for probably the 10th time as I rushed around trying to pick up groceries and the many demands on a list left, as always, on the kitchen table.

With little hope of remembering instructions hastily scribbled on the forgotten scrap of paper, I fielded the inevitable interruptions of 'Are you busy?' Something about those who entered the world of commerce through the dubious arrangement of offering food and a bed for the night to perfect – a debatable choice of adjective there – strangers, in the confines of their own home, drew an insatiable curiosity. The fact the deal was done in exchange for hard cash – preferably – seemed to render the whole operation questionable. What was it, in those early days, that allowed this demanding work to be seen as a way of passing the time, meeting people to while away lonely hours?

'Oh, I didn't think there were that many people about just now,' my new inquisitor ventured, planting herself firmly in my pathway, the implication being I had a hidden cache of paying guests she wanted to know about.

'People?' I airily countered. 'Ah, you mean busy with my guests. No, no visitors about just now at all. Not a single one.'

'Not even singles! That's bad. But I thought you said you were busy.' Her suspicious response was backed by a frown as she cocked her head to the side like an inquisitive sparrow, puzzling over my implied activity.

'I am busy, that I can assure you, and I must be off.'

But Nelly was not to be shifted. She folded her arms across her ample bosom and I sighed, then rushed out an exasperated explanation as to how I could possibly be busy and no people about. People, of course, were not the likes of her or me. People were, in effect, tourists. A torrent of words did not impress upon her the urgency of my busyness, despite hands flying in all directions. 'I have a mountain of paperwork to get through, the garden's like a jungle, there's the family to do for before they do for me, in fact all the mundane chores of the household, and those perverse animals...'

A mutual friend, no doubt attracted by the gesticulations, had the temerity to join us! I could see the ready question forming in her mind, so added for good measure, 'and there's a backlog of telephone calls to catch up with, and probably a hundred emails waiting by the time I get back. And my accountant is threatening me with a tax inspection if I don't get my act together, and the Tourist Board will be only too delighted to chuck me out if I don't get that advertising off tonight!' The natural Highland tendency to gross exaggeration always came to my rescue in times of reeling off why I had no time to stand and stare, or talk of the weather or why 'people' were so scarce, or to indulge in the popular pastime of running down the Tourist Board for diverting business to the west coast – by some pretty devious means – instead of channelling all the 'people' towards the north-east, as they should – the eastern side of the north coast being where I shopped and was frequently accosted to check out my busyness, the west being where I lived, and gleaned my 'people'.

'Oh, that... paperwork... writing, I suppose!' she humphed, not exactly saying rubbish, but one sensed the implication and my hackles rose further. But I was summarily dismissed. Of no further interest. 'I thought you might be busy with people,' and off they strolled, satisfied I was not benefiting from an unfair share of the bed and breakfast market. Her parting shot, wafting over her shoulder, was kindly in tone. 'It'll be busy later no doubt and you'll be glad of having your rest just now.' She couldn't see the black look that followed their ambling departure, oozing a benevolence of time that was theirs to do with as they pleased. I sighed. Making enemies in this line of work was easy enough without offending those who meant me well – but not too well.

From April to October, fondly known to all as 'the season', an affable enquiry after one's health was not the normal greeting, despite a reasonably healthy winter pallor giving way to a near-death's-door whiter shade of pale as the season took its toll, but no matter. The only interest I generated was whether or not I was busy, and being busy actually meant: how many heads are on my pillows?, without the vulgarity of too obvious an interest in my cash flow and emphatically not an interest in how I idled away those dormant hours between serving break-fast and greeting the next stuffed wallet that ambled its way up to my door.

It was firmly believed, and often by the customer who par-took of those very services which took an entire day to provide as much as by those who pondered this source of easy income with no obvious expenditure, that I whittled away the hours of my days twiddling my thumbs, or counting our cash hoard. I took it on the chin because the time to start worrying was when one of the ponderers happened to work for the Inland Revenue, though they were the only ones who credited me with working – my hours of employment not being tax deductible. To all others – neighbours, acquaintances, family and the few friends I had left – I certainly did not work, and therefore was never given the status of a working person.

'Where's Joan working now?' would be politely asked of mother, sister, father, brother. It made no difference, the answer was unanimous, formulated by one and all in the belief I was now a lady of leisure.

'Oh, Joan doesn't work. She just does bed and breakfast.'

'Must be nice for her.' Meaning, it's all right for some.

'Yes. It passes the time for her.' An indulgent answering smile tinged with embarrassment at Joan giving up what was a good career to idle away her hours with bed and breakfast. This would immediately be picked up on and soothed over with an understanding reply: 'Why should she work if she doesn't have to?'

Why? Why, indeed! I've often wondered the whys of it myself, but there was one thing for sure. Work she had to, and work it was, sometimes – most times – involving a 16 hour day; but not in the very beginning, not when those first genuine seekers of good food and comfort found their way to my humble door (or the door I became the proprietor of, as the Tax Man informed me. I didn't feel like a proprietor when I first cautiously approached his den, and felt less like one as I skulked out with my tail between my legs. But he informed me I was a B&B proprietor; well, not exactly; he actually said 'proprietrix'! I had never heard the word before and was ready to relieve the atmosphere with a good giggle, but that was not encouraged.)

Opening the door, my proprietorial door, that auspicious day, I was confronted by a bosom – a very large bosom – commanding so much attention I paid little heed to the stern voice emanating from somewhere above. 'Have you got a room for tonight?'

Much of my youth had been spent in awe of matriarchal

dominance by similarly-endowed women, each given *carte blanche* by my mother to chastise, should the need arise, during those post-war years when the male of the species remained in the service of his country. The women who kept the home fires burning, some actually cutting the peat that fuelled the fires, were made of stern stuff, so even into my middle years the sight of such a well-endowed figure looming large had me back in childhood, scuffing my feet.

I had yet to master the quick lie that would get me out of the alarming prospect of sharing a roof with such mammiferous magnificence, this being the very first week of my venture into bed and breakfast. Such deception required practice, and the possibility of entanglement in plausible lies had to be weighed against the clear advantage it afforded. This was virtually my first enquiry at the door; in the 1960s, the only enquiry you were going to get was one which came at the door. Indeed, we did not aspire to a doorbell that first year, never mind a telephone, with a car being a laughable impossibility. But we, or I should be honest and say I, did have the requisite room.

2

Over My Dead Body

THIS TENTATIVE FORAY into unknown territory was contemplated with the words of my husband of seven years ringing in my ears, when he left his home for the work that would occupy him for decades while we brought up our brand new first-born in the brand new home, built by the not quite so 'new man' who warned, 'It will be over my dead body you take in nighters!'

There is no doubt that, if you want to get somewhere in life, risk-taking is high on the agenda – not that 'taking in nighters', as it was colloquially known, would be likely to get you far at the then going rate of 5/– (all of 25p today, in those days a loaf of bread cost 1/6d, while petrol was 5/2d or 27p per gallon!) for bed and breakfast and 2/6d per person for the high tea that inevitably went with it. (Few, if any, gave a room without offering a meal. Into this, with an on-the-house abandon seldom known today, was thrown the most sumptuous of suppers consisting of copious amounts of tea and masses of home baking. Much of this generosity was to disappear, but for many years it was the accepted and very acceptable norm, even when the proprietor had good reason to suspect some of the hardier types refrained from buying the evening meal so they could sweep the boards at supper time, free of charge.)

In desperation I drew my eyes from the bosom dominating my doorstep and was met with a face every bit as severe as the voice. In panic I thought I would go 'home' for the night, just pack up and run for cover under the roof my siblings and I still called home, though all had flown the nest years ago. But first I would take down that scruffy black and white board, hastily erected by the roadside, advertising my available room.

A flashback to what had happened the very minute that sign went up reinforced my inclination to say 'No!' and pull out of the whole silly idea. The board was barely in place when two people arrived on the doorstep who could be described only as being of the gentry, toffs to their long pale fingertips, the gentleman's tending to steeple, touching beneath his chin as he enquired politely about '...efternoon tea, my deah?' No one had warned me of this possibility, though today we offer what could be termed afternoon tea upon arrival regardless of time of day or evening, but only to those who are committed to staying. This is in the hope of exceeding expectations, though in those early days no such terminology existed as 'expectations', leave alone 'exceeding' them. These were my first actual customers and, despite feeling rather overawed by their grandeur, their confident manner made it seem almost churlish to refuse.

I invited them in.

They did not ask for a room, instead persuading me in the most pleasing manner of their requirement of 'efternoon tea, my deah'. Mesmerised, and having tins brim-full of home baking in anticipation of high teas and suppers, I settled them in what had been our living room but was now 'the guest lounge' and produced what they called a delightful tea, foolishly believing they would eventually ask to see their room and bring in their cases, and kickstart this vision I had of money in my purse.

As it transpired, they were staying at Bettyhill Hotel, in its heyday amongst the finest in the area, where I had spent the year before I married being instructed into the management side of the hospitality industry, though words like 'hospitality' and 'industry' never came into the equation, especially 'industry'. What did I know of industry at 18 years of age! Time spent there had been given over to so much fun and laughter in the close-knit working relationship common to many hotel environments, that for me it was an oasis between secretarial posts, which were much more demanding. This left, in a recess of my mad mind, the impression that looking after the holiday-loving public was by far the most desirable occupation. There sure were a lot of hard truths to learn during a very necessary long arduous apprenticeship, starting off with this posh pair partaking of tea in my lounge. By comparison, secretarial work had been a doddle!

We chatted amicably, and they spent 'such a pleasant efternoon, my deah,' as the gentleman conveyed when he pressed all of sixpence (2½p) into my hand before waving a cheerful goodbye, insisting in his genteel voice that I would do very well with my bed and breakfast venture. I was young enough and silly enough to think it highly funny, exploitation never entering my head, although not in all of the ensuing 40 years was I ever again asked for 'efternoon tea, my deah.'

Himself, the man I married, he of the threatening dead body, had been right. This was not for us. Had I not instinctively felt so when I worked as a secretary years after we married, before our son was born and convention decreed that mums stayed at home, giving up careers to rear the young? A colleague had suggested, 'You could easily do bed and breakfast in your new house.' It was I who threw up hands in horror and mouthed, 'Over my dead body!' Very few couples had the money to build and we were so fortunate that Himself, who was a joiner, had a good friend skilled in the art of bricklaying. They did a reciprocal deal to provide two bungalow homes with little money changing hands, for the simple reason none of us had any. The end result was we each had a home, one we would never have had should money instead of friendship have been the requisite means of barter.

Such progress was viewed with a jaundiced eye by those who believed we had to have a benefactor hidden in the woodwork. As with most youngsters, it was down to us and hard work and forget about the welfare system, which certainly existed then but was scorned by the genuinely needy and exploited by the clever, with most who should have benefited left out in the cold, their pride a poor substitute for their needs.

The excitement of moving into our own home was enhanced by a monumental discovery. 'You're not going to believe this,' I announced breathlessly, reeling from the news myself.

'What have you done now,' said Himself, who, after nearly six years of marriage, was inclined to take such proclamations as the prelude to yet another of my less palatable disasters.

'Ah, I wasn't alone in this one! You played your part too.' I advanced, looking grim.

Blue eyes clocked back and crisp black hair was ruffled as he wondered which escapade had now caught up with him. When my face glowed in unsurpassed happiness, shades of filling in the football coupon or winning the works raffle took hold of him, so I put him out of his misery in case he was disappointed it wasn't news of a bottle of whisky I was about to divulge.

Needless to say, pregnancy after the fun of five years' trying took a bit of grasping and the exciting prospects of new baby and new house kept us planning for months, and here was this colleague of mine suggesting I share it with all manner of strangers. Not on your life!

But a year on, with the new house requiring many new things, and my active nature crying out for something more to do than look after our son, I succumbed to the prodding of those friends who did bed and breakfast, who knew that a connection sited in the prime position of first in the village, along the main route, could be a godsend... to them!

I, of course, was not then aware of the politics of B&B and never envisaged that I would be expected to pass on my overflow, past two of the long-established B&Bs in the village – with their good reputations and detached houses – and into the waiting beds of my friends, whose council home, lovely though it and its garden were, could be frowned upon by the newly-emerging more discerning – undoubtedly snobby, in comparison – visitor. The kindly hospitality and good food that awaited therein soon won them over, but first they had to get there, hence the strategy of positioning a friend on the main route. We did not progress to having colleagues for many a long year, only friends, and as a young new entrant I found nothing but friendship from all of those knowledgeable women. How friendly they were with each other was quite another matter!

Such innocence was certainly a drawback in the early years as I stumbled into the many pitfalls lying in wait for the unwary in this business. But it was also a distinct advantage, for had I known what lay ahead, I would have given it all up there and then, and the man Himself, who regarded such a venture as anathema, would never have known the joys that awaited him when he decided, after retirement from his work on an oil plat-form, to show me how to do the job properly. Nothing new there! By the time Himself set his seal upon the bed and break-fast industry I was well used to being told how to do just about everything by our colleagues from across the border, who saw Scotland as an opportunity to start out anew, selling homes for extortionate prices in the south to buy small hotels or guest houses and B&Bs in the north. Some did a brilliant job, others did not, but they all had this belief that they were the only ones on the planet who knew how to do the job properly.

How I envied them their confidence, whilst biting my tongue at their temerity, especially in later years when we came to realise that the English Tourist Board was not a patch on the Scottish Board, despite our tendency to berate it – though its greatest critics were usually not home-grown.

A special peculiarity, as we saw it, amongst the English

proprietors was their propensity to breakfast with their guests. 'Hospitality should begin in the kitchen,' sighed Mr Guest after being bored out of his skull by the lifetime achievements of his host. 'Yes, and there's times when it should stay there,' agreed his tight-lipped wife, gazing at the congealed breakfast she was too polite to attack in front of the non-eating hosts who sat surveying them with cups of coffee in their hands and a delight in themselves enough to give anyone indigestion. There had been a time, long before the '60s, when mixed breakfasting of family and 'lodgers' was borne of necessity, not from a desire to monopolise and provide so-called early morning entertainment in the name of hospitality.

Such was the gift of achieving a good name under these conditions, it was of intense interest to all and sundry just how one managed this feat of stuffing a stranger in with the family and getting money out of them for what was obviously perceived as little effort. Little effort! Had I known just how much effort was required, I would have missed out on a career that was so underrated those who took it up viewed it as a summer stopgap to pick up pin money, and missed too, one of the best chances going to study the psychology of the human race.

After serving a 20-year apprenticeship, and daring to consider myself fit to push this precarious income stream as a worthy career, about 1988 I began to collar anyone who had influence and insist, 'Look, this is not a lower-end-of-the-market product. You really can make money but you have to provide what the visitor wants!' Said with such conviction, I eventually got the attention and funding required to turn around the opportunities that in time became one of the country's greatest assets when at last tourism was recognised as the economic driver it is today.

Blinkered beginnings kept me in sufficient ignorance to stick to the job that now pays the piper, though I by no means get to choose all the tunes, not without due consultation with Himself – now much more of a 'new man' – who forbade such activities under his roof. It also sees me tearing about the length and breadth of Scotland, improving the tourism product, and in my efforts to keep so many balls in the air, family and friends now get the opportunity to study my antics with raised eyebrows and much muttering behind my back – mind you, human nature, in its helpful desire to inflict consternation upon the person, always sees to it you're made well aware of what's going on behind your back.

At one stage, with Himself away most of the time, a son to care for, as well as two spirited horses, a flock of lambing sheep, a psychologically-challenged house cat and a trio of feline strays, a house rabbit suffering from delusions of identity, all of ten guests, leave alone an increasing number of extra-curricular activities on the tourism front and fitting in appearances at venues with a temperamental guitar as my sidekick, life became somewhat fraught. 'You would think there was no tomorrow,' my mother was prone to announce, shaking her head in bewilderment.

For me, the prospect of no tomorrow became a shocking reality midway through that career. Instead of throwing in the towel as many expected, my prognosis served to focus my mind on all I had yet to achieve in the time left. Today, having owned the first five-star accommodation in the northern counties, with a seat on a handful of boards that would, back then, have seemed ludicrous, I stick out my tongue to the devil that sometimes lurks on my shoulders, whispering, 'How much time have you left?'

'I measure time in quality, not quantity, so piss off... I appreciate you not,' I reply, believing a biblical turn of phrase has a better effect upon the devil that now has Cancer as his capricious assistant. With my half-full cup, and this unshakeable belief that given a fair wind, that cup will never empty – indeed, with a bit of due diligence, may well runneth over – I dismiss my devil... until the next time.

However, due diligence was kind of hard for me to achieve in those early days, and fairness was not always uppermost when it came to heads on pillows, as I was to find out as I progressed from that initial step guided by my friends. Having an excellent eye for the main chance myself, I never blamed them for exploiting my innocence, all such activities later coming under the heading of Marketing Opportunities. But that would be a long time into the future and for the moment I was ready to throw in the towel without having made a penny.

3

Heads on Pillows

JUST AS I WAS about to whinge a denial that I had the desired
room, there bobbed up from behind that overpowering woman,
the jolliest, smiliest face I had ever seen, a veritable Santa Claus
of a face, except there was no white beard. The man behind this
attractive countenance was slight in build, tall, though no taller
than his spouse. Such was his calming impact upon my alarmed
sensibilities that the visions of tearing down the sign and heading
for the sanctuary of 'home' faded fast and, with bated breath,
I offered my one room.

'Well, what do you have for high tea then?' demanded his
formidable other half and my stomach lurched. Little was I to
know that in my answer I was to use the Open Sesame word
that clinched their decision to stay in my home for that night,
which turned into days, and was repeated, season after season,
eventually twice a season and sometimes even thrice, all the way
from the midlands of England, for the next 30-odd years.

Foolishly I thought them old, but they were not, though
eventually frailty did prevent their journeying north and some
years ago a deeply-saddened daughter left behind a broken-
hearted mother to spread the ashes of her father in the sea

below our home, the sea that produced that magic word, when I said, rather shame-faced, 'I'm afraid I have only salmon for tea'; to me common fare, to them manna from heaven.

They were over my doorstep in a flash and from that year on partook of salmon as often as I could produce it. They bought several fish locally every year, to be temporarily entombed in my freezer. They spent the day prior to leaving happily cutting up the fish into coolbox-sized pieces, to be shared with family and friends until they returned. This industry added zest to their holiday, and their camaraderie as they sourced their fish, washed it, ensured it lay flat and straight in the freezer, then cut and bagged for an entire day, was a lesson in contentment and appreciation of needful companionship that eventually gave them pole place amongst our June guests, that special gathering of five couples from diverse parts of Britain who met annually round our dining-room table for more years than can now be remembered.

Now all of those loving couples who not only gave us their valued custom but also their friendship and many lessons in the art of caring, are widowed and their pain is evident through the correspondence we have kept up over the years. The Shrimptons... the Byrnes... the Hamiltons, the Streets, the Bells and so many more. How I miss them. In my gallery of pictures, with its accompanying cheeky comments that still engross guests, there is one photograph of a kitchen ceilidh that depicts many of those precious couples, enjoying piping and dancing performed by my talented nieces. Good memories! Yet, for each good recollection, there is another that may better serve left buried, but in bringing these to the surface the growth of bed and breakfast in Scotland is given an honest airing, and that is where my priority must lie.

My rapport with Dennis Shrimpton was immediate, his unlimited good nature ensuring a constancy of respect that never wavered. I grew extremely fond of Olive Shrimpton too, despite the heaving bosom. But such were those days that it was only in the latter years that I knew them as Dennis and Olive, though I was known to them as Joan, initially due to my youth. Coming from a civil service working environment that insisted upon such formalities, this felt in no way pompous or unfriendly. Indeed, when Americans became part of the bed and breakfast scene, with their passion for first-name terms, I felt such familiarities very strange, as prior to their arrival only the children of guests were known by first names. Now everyone is, just in time to coincide with a degeneration in my mental recall that tests my ability to remember two first names to go with each surname – not forgetting the partners who book into the same room under different surnames. If I get stuck, I refer to them as 'the guests', never 'the nighters', this disparaging term being forced out of favour many years back.

'Nighters' gave way to the word 'people' quite early on in my career. 'Have you any people in tonight?', and you automatically know they're actually thinking 'nighters'. You could be lining yourself up for a mental slap if you were to reply yes, there's people in: yourself, myself, Himself and so on! There was an unbelievable reluctance to use the word 'guest' when enquiring after your situation, yet no such compunction if referring to the occupants of a hotel.

'Guests! Guests? Are you meaning your nighters?' an indignant voice queried as I bought butter at one of the two local shops in the village when I first attempted the alarming task of taking money from people as old as my parents and twice as frightening.

'Put that butter back,' came the outraged demand from behind me. The older woman asked the assistant to give me New Zealand instead. 'That's good enough for them,' she tut-tutted, dismissing the much more expensive Scottish butter as an unnecessary extravagance. She took in people herself, as did so many of the women in the village, and I lacked the nerve to gainsay her. Nevertheless, I had it installed somewhere in my head just exactly what was good for my guests, and cheap NZ butter was not on that list. At least I wasn't pointed in the direction of margarine!

'Did you know, *that* one over the road gives her nighters margarine!' – delivered in hushed outrage, was as good a pointer towards standards as could be had prior to Tourist Board intervention.

It was an instinctive desire to give of the best, and a right lot of trouble it got me into, driving up standards by relentlessly insisting that what the visitor wants, the visitor must get. First though, I had to go through that long apprenticeship, there being so much to learn on an ever-revolving stage.

Both the learning and the constant shifting of goalposts continue 40 years down the line, though at least now I know why the goalposts have to be forever on the move. It's to keep us on our toes and to keep a lot of people in jobs. Changing goalposts is very hard work for the top brass. There's all those meetings to organise and attend, all the sorting out of consultants to seek the view of the trade to be sure it's done from a 'bottom-up' perspective. Then there's all the analysis to be carried out and sister agencies to be conferred with before the trade is told where next to place the ball, but, by the time the trade starts to manoeuvre the ball into position, the top brass have already begun to think of changing the goalposts once again. It keeps a lot of people totally occupied and adds many new phrases to the vocabulary, such as 'green tourism', alongside many new expletives some of us didn't even know we had stored in the recesses of our minds.

In the beginning there was no overseer whatsoever and you did what you thought best, until onto the scene came the Scottish Tourist Board, which was hailed with a curiosity akin to a cat poking at a mouse to see which way it would jump. The board's ideas were good, would bring lots of visitors to your area, and it had the means through which you could actually entice those visitors right to your door, if you paid it a subscription fee and advertising money. Sounded great. It did bring more visitors to the area, and to the doors of not just the members but the non–members alike. That would have been the first fly in the ointment. When the visitor headed for the door across the street which paid nothing for the privilege, then neighbour began to view neighbour with distrust, and laid all the blame on the innocent shoulders of the newly emerging Tourist Board. With the increased trade came the increased discontent. It became apparent, now there was an identifiable body such as the Scottish Tourist Board to which a visitor could report back, that some places were far from being satisfactory, so on to the scene marched the board's fledgling Quality and Standards Scheme. It was a bold step, and the right step. Someone, somewhere, had to keep an eye on us!

Just recently, in the monthly column I write for one of the newspapers, I expounded upon the shock many visitors get when they come across a stunning lack of service, writing of a young girl, familiar with hotel work, who started in a hotel run for a time by proprietors new to the hospitality industry. 'You'll have it easy today,' she was told. 'There's no one leaving this morning.' She immediately offered to service the rooms. Her boss looked at her as if she were mad. 'You don't go near rooms when people are staying on.'

This unbelievable situation was created in ignorance of hotel practice, not in a desire to dodge the needs of the visitors. Guests who had stayed at another hotel were astounded to be asked, 'Do you want your rooms serviced when you're out?'

Anyway, this morning, with staggered breakfasts – which is unusual at our B&B, it being marketed on the ambience created when all our visitors sit round the table together and have what is generally construed as a whale of a time – I was slightly disorientated while doing the cleaning. Happily putting away the gear, I thought myself very clever to be so ahead with the work. The sun was shining and I had my eye on a lounger abandoned yesterday when duty called. I happened to glance at the closed door of Room 2. I had forgotten all about it. The guests were staying on while all others had left early and this had merrily slipped my mind; the memory playing some fine tricks on me, which I know is down to the addition of something peculiar to the water supply and nothing to do with age, for aren't the young nowadays just as afflicted by this blight on mental capacity?

I thought, how awful if I'd completely forgotten, which I might well have done, essential tasks fly out of my head for hours on end until something alerts the senses. Just imagine, the very thing I wrote against with censure so recently would have faced my own guests upon their return!

Then I sighed a sigh of relief, for that could never happen now. Like T. S. Eliot's Cat of the Railway Trains, I have my very own Skimbleshanks behind me, ready to remind me, to ensure that nothing dreadful can go wrong. The man Himself was bearing down, key in hand, attending to his end of the bargain set after his retirement amicably enough, when a natural division of labour came about; after a few initial contretemps, that is.

4

Going into Season

I USED TO ONLY take in a few couples during the week, covering the sad-looking small white board on which I had painstakingly painted 'Bed and Breakfast' in bold crooked black letters to welcome Himself home at weekends to a visitor-free house, not bothering about dead bodies and such like threats.

Being young and carefree, I loved social occasions, most of which in this area centred round the dances that all except the infirm and the newly born graduated towards. As children we were taught different dances by our elders and encouraged on to the floor, before being persuaded home long before the social occasion drew to its early morning conclusion. Permission to go dancing was easier to win when dances were preceded by concerts, which were real family affairs. Official ceilidhs came later; they began with everyone doing a turn, be it by mouth or by instrument, followed by a dance, with as much emphasis on Gaelic music as on the waltzes, set dances and reels, performed by accordion players, fiddlers and pipers, with no sign of a guitar in those far-off days.

The concerts of our youth were exciting events. Younger artists gave of their best in the first half, which always ended with a sketch, and the main play was performed in the second. The interval was used for setting up the stage and sneaking a sly dram, the halls being dry. The concert ended about 11 pm, after which the hall would be cleared, swept out and prepared for the dance. Sad to say the arrival of the large construction squads who built the atomic energy site nearby put paid to children being encouraged to many dances, as the bold lads took to engaging in fisticuffs with the local men – as well as certain of the women, who could give as good a hand-bagging as Margaret Thatcher ever did!

Some localities had a reputation for wild dances, others for real social occasions. The Straths were not so popular with the itinerant and meaner elements of society, ensuring a good time could be had regardless of age. Anyone of worth in a community belonged to the hall committees who ran these occasions; indeed the heart of a village beat to the skills of those colourful personalities who provided most of the entertainment, some a little more directly than others, along the entire coastline.

It was the occasion of one of these dances in a nearby Strath that set the seal upon my tentative testing of the bed and breakfast waters. I covered the sign that Friday, just before Himself arrived home, set my eight-month-old son in a push-chair and headed for the shop, one mile away.

Returning, I sang in happy oblivion as I shoved my way up our bumpety dirt-track brae, ready to greet the breadwinner, knowing he would have been dropped off by workmates home for the weekend. In fact there was still a car outside the garden gate. I could hear Himself whistling in the garage; he never whistled, not unless he was up to no good.

I approached warily, expecting to find him with the owner of the car, searching out an elusive tool from the conglomeration of implements lining the walls and floor of the garage. It had been built precisely to store such things, the possibility of our owning a car being extremely remote.

He was on his own, and whistling tunelessly.

What could be wrong? It could have nothing to do with the covered sign arrangement as that had been in place for several weeks. I had got his acceptance on that issue, retroactively I admit. You needed your husband's agreement in those days, especially if you married a man almost 10 years your senior who kept his nose to the grindstone while you were playing at keeping house. He was not alone in his male abhorrence of this practice of turning one's home into a B&B, which saw many a man ousted from his comfortable spot at the fireside or the head of the table so that strangers could be seated and dined in comfort. For Himself, the comfortable fireside was of no attraction, nor was head of the table, as he had neither a dominant nature nor time for idling; he just did not take to strangers. That was the problem.

The understanding was that at no time, none whatsoever, would I take in these frightening people when he was at home. I had kept the bargain, even when it meant not seeing a penny most of the week and having to turn away a lovely couple the nights he was home. I virtuously, and without complaint, refused any who offered their lure of lucre in favour of honouring my side of the bargain. A few martyr-like sniffs and comments of how handy the money would be may have passed my lips, and envious remarks made on the cars of visitors strewing the village and me with my sign all covered up. Regardless, a deal was a deal and I kept to it.

I had called at his mother's and arranged for her to babysit. We were to join friends and head for a dance in the Strath after dinner. We didn't go out often and I was as excited as a child at the prospect, though I have to admit Himself was never so enthused and would often sidle out of an event, leaving me to join his sisters and friends while he went home to work on the house. Invite him to the pub for a pint though and there was no prevarication, so long as it was the male bastion of good craic and not the cocktail lounge, where couples sat together. Women were not encouraged to enter the male preserve of the public bar, unless invited in to sell raffle tickets, and that at their own risk: the all-male company would vie with each other to treat us with tremendous respect, which had to include generosity of spirit. And if we weren't prepared to partake of the spirits then we shouldn't have set foot in *their* bar.

I peeked round the back door of the garage, to be met with his sheepish grin as I called out, 'Whose car is that?'

'Well,' came the evasive reply, 'There's people in the house wanting to see you,' and with a flick of a switch, a heavy-duty drill drowned out all attempts at an inquisition. He had ways of handling situations.

Smelling a rat, I rushed through the kitchen and opened the living-room door. Sitting on our three-seater couch, feet barely touching the floor, backs formidably straight, hands folded in laps and heads cocked in unison for all the world like three brown hens on a perch, sat three little old ladies.

'Oh, my dear,' said the first one, 'your husband is so kind.'

'Oh, yes, my dear,' her friend breathlessly cut in, 'we were so afraid we had rather taken too much of a chance.'

'Oh, indeed, we had,' clucked the third. 'He is such a lovely man.'

Is he, I thought, still smiling, with the baby in one arm. Without further ado, they flocked towards the child and oohed and aahed in proper appreciation of a sleeping infant – especially of one whose roof you intend sharing that night. 'Yes my dear, your friends who could not put us up said you had a baby but you also had just what we wanted.' She glanced coyly at her companion, indicating her turn to continue this one-sided, or should that be three-sided, conversation.

'Your lovely kind husband said it would be no problem for us to stay, so long as we all shared the one room. He so kindly showed it to us and it is just perfect.'

I knew it. I just knew it, the minute I heard the whistling.

I would kill him later. We had only one room available in our three-bedroom house back then, the guest room with three single beds and no hot and cold running water, guests using the family bathroom just across the corridor. I shared a room with Himself and the baby had the third, lovingly prepared as a nursery long before his arrival. My mother, a good paperhanger, took unusual exception to the duck-patterned yellow and blue paper that prohibited its use as a guest room. The paper, she said, was not patterned straight – for she dare not accuse the walls of being a fraction out, with the man Himself having built the house and thus being sensitive to any such insinuation. His reputation for perfection in his work went well before him, ensuring all complaints were laid squarely at my door. I had made a bad choice of wallpaper.

Another room was still piled up with wood and tools and odds and ends; it was eventually to become our sitting room when I cottoned on that guests did not really care to share a lounge with the family and were happier when they knew they had their own relaxation area. I was recognising the worth of deals and sticking to them. Pity was, those I dealt with had no such compunctions.

'You're allowing them use of your own living room to themselves?' came exasperated exclamations from family, friends and especially B&B wifies, horrified at the thought I should encourage such ideas of largesse. The expectation with some was that 'nighters' should leave the premises in the morning and not come back until evening, and then stay in their rooms after high tea, with a bit of luck not to be seen again until breakfast time. Other, more good-hearted souls – and there were many – encouraged strangers into their living rooms rather than to stay in a bedroom and did so with great sincerity, and many a good ceilidh emanated from such practice. But having a completely separate lounge for the guests was not always on the cards before the '50s, though by the end of the '60s my inspirational attitude had become the norm.

My three little hens, clucking in harmony, proceeded to put the kibosh on my evening out.

'My dear, your lovely husband said we would be able to partake of your advertised high tea.' And that was it. I cancelled the babysitting, which meant a quick run up the road as there was no telephone to hand for the first few years. Then I set about feeding us all. That lovely kind man had the audacity to wander back in with a big grin on his face, but I soon wiped it off.

'Yes, fine, we can stay in and not go to the dance, but never again will I cover the sign just because you are due home,' I declared with the tenacity of an animal scenting victory. It was open season. He had deliberately taken in these ladies and his feeble entreaties of how could he turn away these sweet little dears and us with just what they wanted were brushed aside and a new pact took over.

On the Sunday night, before taking leave of his dangerously defiant wife and baby son, not forgetting his dear little ladies who had decided he was so lovely they would stay longer, he studiously sat down with a board he had cut and painted gleaming white, ready to meticulously scribe the appropriate 'Bed and Breakfast', under which was lettered the much-sought-after 'High Tea'. It was highly superior to my effort, which, he said, was a total embarrassment.

Within an hour of setting up the sign at the end of the driveway we had enquirers at the door. He was proud as punch. You would think the whole idea had been his. But we were firmly committed now and from that day on, though he avoided all direct contact with the scary guests, he was my greatest sup-porter. He agreed to my needs for another room, hot and cold running water in the bedrooms, and central heating and double glazing throughout the house. You name it, I thought of it, and he, if it were feasible at all, got the job done. What a team! But it was not that easy. And of course, the more I achieved for the comfort of my precious guests, the more I wanted.

5

John Dear and the Rabbit

AS THE GUESTS SLOWLY streamed in, the pennies mounted and I made my first serious purchase. The last room in the house was gutted out and the finest Axminster I could lay hands on was fitted. I loved that carpet. There was no money over for furniture, but we had the carpet. It would never have worn out, but in time it came to a rather unpleasant end, leaving me to mourn its loss and fail to find its equivalent. I vowed to keep the room as a sitting room, having already installed a bed-settee on the bare floorboards in order to let not just one room to guests but two. I stowed our clothes in boxes in the hall cupboard and commandeered part of the tall-boy in the baby's room.

We saw a great many families holiday in the area, with most B&BS offering family rooms, and if happy, those families returned year after year until the children grew up. Many a child's card winged our way, addressed at times to The House of the Black Rabbit, the postman knowing full well where the black rabbit lived.

Our nearby town had got its first pet shop and I took my small god-daughter Joan there for a visit. We were both enthralled by the animals, particularly by a family of tiny black bunnies ready for homing, all long ears and feet heavily furred like dark-brown felt slippers. 'Rex rabbits,' the man in charge informed us, 'Much more like hares in their looks, but they are rabbits.'

'Please can I get one?' came the earnest entreaty, and knowing her family's love of animals I risked a yes. Into a small brown paper bag was popped one tiny rabbit. I was charmed with it and probably more excited than the child. For when we exited the shop, passing cages of smelly, multi-coloured mice, babies and parents scurrying about in a manner likely to put any sensible person off owning one, Joan stopped dead in her tracks, her face lit with wonder.

'I would love a baby mouse.' I stared with mounting horror at this tiny scrap of pink and black baldness, huge round ears sticking up behind black beady eyes. It was unquestionably ugly. Words to the effect of 'You cannot be serious' and 'Oh yes I am' passed quickly between us.

Five minutes later we left the shop, each clutching a little brown paper bag. I hadn't the heart to put the bunny back.

My little namesake arrived home with her pet, which she nursed and adored and never lost interest in until it died of old age years later. She called it Thomas. But, frequent though my visits were, I never took to it. Instead, I became the owner of one of the first house rabbits we ever knew of, long before they became a must-have fashion item. We had no facilities other than the house for this delightful little scamp, who never in the years we had him chewed or scraped anything inside the house, allowing me the illusion that all rabbits behaved in like manner.

Only the other day, at the first ever conference in Scotland dedicated to B&B owners, I sat with a man who had once stayed at The Sheiling. His abiding memory was of sitting in our lounge with this black rabbit lying sleeping at his feet. What really surprised him was that the rabbit ruled the roost over the cat and the dog.

The rabbit was christened by our son, who would have

been about a year old and was the proud owner of a large Bugs Bunny bendy toy, which were all the rage then. 'What 'at?' he asked, as little children do when they discover the value of the question. 'It's a little bunny rabbit,' I told him. 'Not,' said he, gazing at the long ears, remarkably similar to Bugs Bunny's. ''Sa Bendy.' And Bendy it was.

The other occupant of the house was not near so thrilled, and I don't mean Himself, who was speechless to come back and find a rodent well ensconced in his home. I'm talking about Roxy, my terrier dog, who was used to chasing wild rabbits, having a whole croft to roam and plenty of hill-walking opportunities, and resented the intrusion of one into his home.

One fine sunny day, not a guest in sight, Bendy and I lay in a patch of grass near the back door that, at a stretch, you could call a back green, sunning ourselves while I introduced the tiny rabbit to the joys of romping about outside. Though Roxy disliked Bendy, he had never threatened him in any way and it was with some surprise we saw the dog arrive back from one of his many forays into the hill ground with a very small, very dead, baby rabbit, which he must have taken from a nest. I was most put out, this being something he had never done before.

Soon he arrived and dumped the second baby down beside us, and the third and the fourth. He could easily see my distress though Himself grumbled, 'What do you expect? He's a terrier dog and it's you who took him here despite all I said about it being a very bad idea.' Yes, I remembered all that, and all the recrimination that went with it, but I had been two months married and foolishly thought my mere whim would be met with a natural desire to please. We were living, courtesy of his Uncle Jock, on a croft holding a flock of lambing sheep cared for by a collie dog and the proposal to introduce a terrier puppy threw their hands up in a united front of dissuasion. I brought the puppy home and negotiated terms afterwards.

But Roxy never laid tooth or claw on the rabbit as he grew

into a particularly fine specimen, and Bendy got his own back on the dog by spitting and growling at him whenever he deemed it necessary, making a point of removing him from his favourite place across the hearth and lying there himself. The dog would slink under the writing bureau, giving black looks to all and sundry. We called it skooking out from under, thus Roxy became forever known as Skooker.

That kind of peculiar behaviour from a rabbit, albeit a very large buck rabbit, might have been OK with the resident dog, but in those days we still let our guests bring their own pets into the house, once having to negotiate our way round an iguana whilst doing the clearing up.

'Oh, you've got a rabbit,' a rather pernickety lady gasped as she came into in the lounge. 'Maybe you should put it back in its hutch. John will be bringing the dog through in a moment.'

I explained that this was our pet, a resident rabbit, and he had never lived in a hutch, the fields and the hills being his territory, where he bossed about a colony of wild rabbits and chose his own doe from amongst them. The house, to which he had access whenever he wished, was his 'hutch'.

'He seldom stays out at night, always keeping roughly to the hours of the dog.'

'A dog? You have a dog as well as a rabbit, living in the house?' She looked quite perplexed.

'Skooker's not at home. He just comes and goes as he pleases, visiting my in-laws. He's visiting his friends at the moment, three elderly ladies he goes to see. He never misses out on a Wednesday, the day the butcher's van is on the go, but he's in here by evening time and funnily enough the rabbit is inclined to come home from the hills then too.'

'But we must be careful our dog doesn't harm the rabbit, mustn't we, John dear?' She patted the couch for John dear to sit down beside her, and pass a wheezing King Charles onto her lap.

Cue the rabbit. He sat staring at them for a time, particularly watching the dog, then as other guests gathered he approached John dear and his wife, whose name I now forget.

'Oh, isn't he sweet?' she enthused as he allowed himself to be stroked. Then without warning he got up on his hind legs in a startlingly menacing position and shot out his front paws in boxer style, spitting from the back of his throat. Low guttural growling noises filled the room as sharp claws slashed the air in a very threatening manner. The recipients of this display were no longer amused and John dear was asked to remove their darling dog to the safety of the bedroom. The rabbit and I got looks to match his colour for the rest of the night.

Dogs were no contest for the bold lad. They either removed themselves or were removed by shocked owners. Then Bendy would retire, satisfied, to the front of the fire, to be admired by those who appreciated this territorial display, which could easily have lost me a star had such ratings been in effect then. He was a character; his lifestyle, his warren, his favourite doe and his long fight back from myxomatosis – he was the first rabbit on record to be nursed through and survive that most odious of diseases – made him a vital part of our lives. The few years he graced our home gave not only me but our guests, and particularly their children, an insight into the ways of a creature far different from what our imaginations and ignorance have led us to believe.

My brother, a Navy man with a keen love of reading, arrived unexpectedly from London one day, saying, 'Hey, I saw this book with a rabbit on the cover and thought you might like it. Started reading it on the train and couldn't put it down.' It was a very solid thick paperback and after a few pages I gave up. I just could not read such rubbish and wondered if my sibling had taken leave of his senses.

As the weeks passed, I saw more and more of the very same book, *Watership Down*, lying on guests' bedside cabinets and when winter approached I grabbed the book again. After the first chapter I was hooked. I have seldom read a book I enjoyed as much as that one. I would never have believed I, then a non-fiction reader, could enjoy a novel so much, but Richard Adams's insight into the life of the rabbit was so realistic in everything that Bendy had taught me as he lived out his life on the land surrounding our home.

When obliged by the law not to let Bendy out to mix with the wild rabbits while he had myxomatosis – which is ironic considering he was infected by them – I had to purchase a harness and lead to give him a walk. Until he got too ill, he was adamant he did not want to use an inside toilet, so on would go the harness and off we would set. In comparison with kittens, who had to learn the Green Cross Code, and Roxy when a pup, Bendy was brilliant on the harness and lead, a light felt contraption made for a small cat. The guests took special delight in seeing him set off on his walks, though it caused an element of doubt to creep into the minds of new arrivals. Were they to put up with this daft young girl who was taking a rabbit out for a walk? Was it really she who would cook their meal and see to their comfort all the time they were staying? Their faces said it all, but hearing of his illness changed their concern for themselves into concern for the recovering bunny, and most were charmed with his antics and determination to live.

Bendy took me to rocks, or old tuffets of peat, which, from the amount of rabbit droppings on them, were his toilets, and only on these particular spots would he sit for ages adding to the pile. This and many other examples of the genuine behaviour of rabbits in the wild are given throughout *Watership Down*, adding to its allure. When I finally and very reluctantly turned over the last page, I cried, not just over the death of Hazel-rah but because I had finished the book.

My own first novel was written long, long after reading *Watership Down* and though the main characters are animals and it involves a journey of discovery, I don't recollect even thinking of *Watership Down* whilst writing. There are no other similarities in the entire book, and to attempt to emulate the writing of so eminent an author as Richard Adams would have been foolish in the extreme. The publishers, when putting out a press release on *The Land Beyond the Green Fields*, said the book was in the 'spirit' of *Watership Down*, which may well be true, but they are two very different tales, told from very different perspectives.

When Bendy first contracted myxomatosis, my love for him could not allow me to have him put to sleep so long as there was a chance. By coincidence, the veterinary practitioners had become interested in the possibilities of developing a vaccination for pet rabbits against this most sinister of diseases. The local vet assured me that very often it was dedicated and loving nursing that saved an animal if the disease in itself was not fatal. With wild rabbits, it was their inability to see as well and hear, and often to feed, that ensured their sad end. If I were willing to give it a go, he would supply the medication and treatment free of charge, if he could use the case at a lecture he was to give at Aberdeen University.

My rabbit recovered well from the disease but was left with a distinctive reminder. On the middle of one large black ear, two back-to-back pustules had healed into the usual hard lumps, which dropped off leaving a little round hole as if he were lug marked. This was one of only two differences in him after nine long weeks of nursing and caring.

The other was a change of character, which puzzled me. It was not that he became soft. He proved that the first day he went out and I saw the great welcome given by his friends from the warren on the hill, those who had survived the onslaught of myxomatosis, amongst them Star, his female companion, who appeared to have been immune.

'Look,' I called Himself, all excited. There were Bendy and another big, wild rabbit at the back fence, leaping like hares into the air. One or two other rabbits were dancing about. 'Look at the great welcome they're giving each other.' Within minutes I had guests in the kitchen, all looking out the back window rejoicing in the delight of the rabbits.

'That's no welcome. That's a fight!' said Himself, not amused at the intrusion, which he knew from past experience would have him trapped answering questions for the duration of the daylight, and him with a million jobs to do outside.

I looked more closely and saw tufts of fluff flying. Then I was flying myself, out the door and up the hill, with Himself in hot pursuit. 'Leave them alone. He'll sort it out and he won't thank you.' He was laughing though. It gave him his chance for escape.

Bendy was soon back in command of his warren. But he didn't stay out near so much and was inclined to hop onto my knee for stroking at every opportunity. He no longer put Skooker off his perch and took little interest in guest dogs. He was as big and healthy as ever and had been given a clean bill of health. He still had the occasional romp with Glen, the sheepdog belonging to Himself's Uncle Jock, so I believed all was well.

The end of the season came and, with Neil, I took the train down to my sister Muriel's for a short break, as Himself was to be home for a long weekend. We were by then the divided owners of a brand new blue minivan – divided in that it was his pride and joy and I hated it. All my life I wanted a car and when we could afford a new one what did he want? A bloody minivan. Still, it was wheels and it afforded freedom for many things, not least visiting family, all of whom had young children now. We were to stay in Inverness a couple of days and Himself was to drive down to collect us. The day before, he telephoned to ask how I was getting on.

'How is Bendy?' Top priority.

'He's fine as far as I know. And so am I.'

'What do you mean, as far as you know?

'He's never come into the house since you left.'

'Right, that's it. You can come down for us today instead of tomorrow. I have to come home now.'

And he did, but a dreadful storm came that night and he and his brother-in-law decided to go out for 'just a pint'. Just a pint takes much, much longer to drink than a normal pint and I should have known. Hours later it was too late and really far too wild a night for me to drive north, just a pint putting him beyond taking a wheel between his hands, so we stayed while I worried about Bendy, but I knew he had lots of cosy out-houses to go to, one of his favourites having all the winter hay stored in it.

The minute we got home, I was out on the croft calling him. Then Jock made his way towards me, grim faced. His words have stuck with me ever since. 'You needn't be looking for that rabbit of yours. He's lying dead by the old byre door.'

The bottom dropped out of my world. I was stunned. It wasn't lack of pity, just the old man's way. He was fond of the rabbit and greatly amused whenever Glen and Bendy played catch as catch can, the dog never managing to catch the agile rabbit, but never trying that hard, enjoying the weave of the chase too much. Jock said he did not know what was wrong. The second his back turned I raced into the house and up to my room, where I cried my eyes out. I could not bring myself to go and take the rabbit home, but Himself did, and said there was no mark whatsoever on him.

'He was beside the entrance to the byre with all that hay in it. He could have gone in if he wanted.' Nothing could console me. It had been such a short time ago that we – the district nurse, who was attending me for anaemia and had weekly inspected Bendy to see how he was doing, much more interested in his progress than mine; my mother, who, despite his wicked ways with her, was buoyant when she saw the first signs of his recovery; the vet, who was jubilant to announce to students how the rabbit had fully recovered; another nurse, who surreptitiously supplied me with pads to use for his toilet when he was going through the worst stages of the disease; his various visitors; and many others – had been so pleased at his long-awaited recovery. So short a time ago that I had plucked the last rose from the garden to give him a treat, his mouth still sore and the dandelions in decline. Watching him eat petal after velvety pink petal, knowing he was really going to get better, the euphoria of getting his life back so contrasted with the despair of his sudden death, unaccounted for even by the vet, who could only say that the illness might have left him physically weak.

For a time, cards continued to arrive addressed to The House of the Black Rabbit.

6

The Year of the Sheep

THE SHEEP WERE with us much longer than a year, though for me the intensity of involvement was spasmodic. I hated sheep. They are the only animal I can say I ever actively disliked, never had and never wanted anything to do with, but needs must when the devil drives. My avid cries of 'over my dead body!' have always had little effect upon the way our lives have evolved.

We were given the croft land our house stands on by the uncle we stayed with for the first six years of our marriage. This uncle kept sheep and I kept my distance – from the sheep, not Jock, with whom I got on extremely well, despite first impressions.

The man not yet known as Himself – you have to have status to be known as Himself within a household – had dragged me from a wedding dance to meet his uncle, me all of 18 years and dolled up to the nines. 'Best foot forward,' said my fiancé, keen to make a good impression as he ushered me in the door of the place soon to become our home, past jute sacks of sheep feed stacked in the front porch.

I looked down at the best foot I could offer, clad in its spiky four-inch-heeled sandal, stepping into this predominantly male preserve, and realised the impression I gave might well be true, but it would not be good! I looked nothing like a crofter's wife, and why should I? I was not marrying a crofter, just a chap who happened to have a crofter uncle. But Jock proved a patient man who did not judge a book by its cover.

Living there on the land indicated some kind of commitment and as Himself had a hankering after keeping some sheep, when Jock was warned by advancing years to stop chasing after his flock of rather petted breeding ewes, he sold out but kindly gave over to us a couple of his favourite pets. We then bought from his lady friend – they eventually married when he reached the ripe old age of consent at 81 years – a few more well-cared-for creatures to allow us the nucleus of a breeding flock. I say 'us', but it was Himself really, and the threat of dead bodies was lost in his enthusiasm. By then I had a baby to care for and plans that I am reminded I instigated and carried out '...behind my back for long enough until I cottoned on and made you that sign before I set off for Orkney!' His cottoning-on probably had a mercenary side, when I think of it, as by then there must have been some evidence of my coping and earning some money to plough back into our many needs.

It was his departure to the Orkney Islands, leaving me with his small flock for weeks on end, that began my initiation into the real reasons why any sensible person should shy away from keeping hill sheep – any sheep – deranged, obstinate creatures that they are. Except for my pet lambs, that is: born with immense intelligence, winning ways and the ability to look cute and cuddly in their creamy, curly coats. I passionately cared for their well-being.

My dislike of sheep was intensified a few years earlier when Roxy was very young. During lambing, he became close friends with Bimbo, the offspring of Uncle Jock's favourite sheep – all being pets, he had to have favourites. The lamb and pup spent hours romping about in the garden, as the mother was allowed in to eat the succulent grass, helping her milk production. One day she took extreme exception to the friendship, got Roxy up against a stone dyke and the corner of the peat stack and gave him a right duffing. He really was hurt, though quickly rescued by us when we heard his screams of distress. I now knew for sure sheep were a bad lot. My well-brought-up canine was immediately banned from entertaining such ruffians in the garden, but the old man insisted the dog had learned a good lesson: keep away from sheep! Would that I had been allowed the same lesson.

In those early days, being left with the flock proved little problem as Jock still had his dog Glen, who became close friends with Bendy and his successors. Yet for some reason he killed one of two guinea pigs belonging to my friend Anne's daughter while I, an obvious capable animal lover, was entrusted with their care. I just about died of mortification when the child came bouncing back from holiday early to find only one of her precious pets left. Try explaining that without breaking a tender heart, not to mention a friendship.

The April after the B&B sign was officially erected saw me tackle my first lambing. I did not impress. But I loved it, out there in the fields and on the hills as glorious sunrises brightened a morning that echoed with the lively bleat of springing lambs. Often I mused as I sat in our wide window watching the intricate and exciting games devised by the leaders of the teams, how come they turned into stupid, staid sheep in so short a time? But sheep were not stupid and though we kept our own well away from the newly-erected garden paling, I despaired as I watched various neighbours' animals fly over our fences and help themselves to anything that flourished.

Our sheep were petted and everywhere that Uncle went, the sheep were sure to go, which made lambing fairly easy. But he insisted I be the one to deliver the difficult births. He was, as were all those Campbell brothers, a big man, and his hands were huge. He had, to his credit, a sensitivity to the ewes' discomfort and preferred me to use my smaller hands. When, through his instructions, I presented sufficient of the new lamb for him to grip, he would do the necessary pulling while I empathised with the grunting mother. It always amazed me how sympathy and stroking the head appeared to alleviate distress – mine as much as hers, as I found this business very hard on a mind that remembered the pangs of birth only too well. It was OK for the males. The tup was long gone to his 10-month holiday on lush pastures, and the men who kept the flocks and lambed the sheep would have taken to the hills at the merest prospect of attending the birth of one of their own offspring!

At that time, we never dreamt of calling out a vet, not with the wealth of knowledge and ability available in most of the adjacent croft houses. I learned how to manoeuvre the confusing mass of limbs within the womb of the sheep but often had tremendous difficulty in pulling out the lamb, mostly because I was terrified of harming it. It was years before that expert stockman, Colin MacKenzie, taught me the value of heeding the contractions and working with the mother to ease the lamb out. When successful, especially if alone, the absolute euphoria is indescribable. I soon began to stamp my ownership on certain newborns.

'That one is mine!' I would proudly point at various lambs as they were gathered for tail docking, castration, dosing, medicating and every other one of the jobs that kept you on the land most weeks right through until they sailed off in the lorries in August to their inevitable end. The night after the sale allowed none to sleep, as you were kept awake by the crescendo of heartbreaking cries from the mothers and remaining siblings. The cream of the flock, if female, were kept to breed with and each year I prayed my favourite animal would produce at least one first-class ewe lamb so she would not end the summer mourning her loss.

It became obvious that sustainability would require a higher commitment, considering the growing demands of the government regarding stock and the upkeep of crofting lands, so I negotiated a deal I believed would work in my favour, whilst Himself was as confident it would work to his benefit. He, and the Crofters Commission, wanted more sheep on the land. I wanted more understanding from him towards my horses. By the time it became obvious Troubie my son's pony needed a stable companion, I had a taste for the joys found on the back of a horse. I desperately wanted my own horse and spent an entire summer looking for the right one. That I landed with the wrong one is due to my ignorance and the ability to be won over and completely charmed by an animal who says he is really nice, kind, loyal and ready to do your bidding at the drop of a whip – provided it was not on his flank.

'I would never dream of hitting you,' I crooned as I flung my arms round his neck the day I found him, after a six-hour drive and a fatal falling in love, as Himself inspected the ripped jacket resulting from the first of the many altercations between them. The field we left him in had a low hill in its centre and as we drove off, he raced to the top, tail flying and head held high, watching us out of sight.

It was a striking picture and I wondered why anyone would call such a beautiful animal by a common name like Bronco. Only too soon I was to find out. Horse riding in our area had ended long years ago and Troubie was the first pony to join the community in decades, most people wondering if we had taken leave of our senses. I had this idea that a child should grow up with an animal to love and care for, and a pony would give him 20 years or more of interest and companionship, keeping him away from the inevitable lure of the pub, there being little else of indoor entertainment in the entire village. But in the long run I kept neither the child nor the horses out of that particular establishment.

Entertainment was certainly available for the guests, what with Felix and her bunnies, Bronco and Troubie and their competitive displays, and the sheep. The flock grew and developed through times that proved in the end too demanding to sustain, when the uncle became too old to help and the worthies with their knowledge followed suit, leaving me wondering where to turn in times of stress. The flock-master was now earning his living in the North Sea out on the oil rigs, working away for two weeks and spending a precious two at home caring for the flock.

Bronco was not what he said he was when I tried him out, except in one respect which caused much of the early angst between him and Himself, who had welcomed him onto the croft despite the torn jacket. The horse was loyal to a fault. He was adamant I belonged to him and that Troubie would do as he was told, despite the pony having been extremely friendly to him, inviting Bronco into the field off the lorry after his long, long journey and taking him into his stable, allowing him the best loose-box, anything he liked. And Bronco sure liked his own way, taking command and lead role instantly. But it was his attitude to me that irked everyone. He was not an easy horse to ride but was a beauty, who rose to the saddle and showed off his part-thoroughbred breeding to great advantage. We had hoped his Highland genes would ensure we had an animal with the temperament necessary for an inexperienced rider like myself. Neil was not quite six and just backing Troubie when Bronco arrived.

We already knew we should not have given a nine-month-old part-Arab foal to a four-year-old child, who had to wait two years to even sit on his back, leave alone break the animal for riding. But the time together ensured a lifetime bond. Bronco was not a horse for a beginner, but he wanted me, I wanted him, and we got what we wanted, with temper tantrums on both sides, fun, worry, rows, a learning curve unimaginable, ecstatic days in the saddle, nightmare times, vet bills galore, long hours together at one with each other, groomings that ended in tears, shoeings when he bit me first then I bit him, hard, and he never did it again. Nor did I, the taste of dust and hair in my mouth lasted for hours, but it taught us both a lesson. Learning to ride on an animal like that taught me all about hitting the ground running, though he did the running and I did the hitting.

Bronco arrived with a passion for beer, but it had to be Tennent's Tartan, with his own bowl at the pub. He quickly developed a drug habit when he discovered nettles. Our croft was full of them. He dug up the roots, cleaned them on stone dykes, making heaps of the tubers, which he would stand over and chew contentedly for hours on end, offering some to Troubie, who refused, being a clean-living pony and not into that sort of thing. Soon Bronco would be swaying on his feet, eyes glazed, on a trip he wished to share with none. We never discovered the properties that encouraged his addiction, but he cleared the croft of nettles during his lifetime.

But first he continued getting on the wrong side of the one person he should have won over. We three set off for the beach. I rode first and all went remarkably well. Then Himself went to get in the saddle. You would think we were going to kill him, the horse. He went hysterical. No way was that man getting on his back; indeed, after we got him calmed down he wanted nothing whatsoever to do with that man, and he advised me to be of the same inclination. This was difficult for me but each time Himself dared to come near me, he was head-butted off or I was circled round so he couldn't get close to me. Then my 'friend' decided I should not have anything to do with Troubie either, and when this jealousy was extended to my child, I knew I had to master his possessiveness. This was accomplished in time, but the damage was done.

To Himself he became That Horse, though to me he was the wonderful Bronco, and to our son, Your Horse. It was not a good starting point but I spent hours caring for him, assuring him I loved him to bits, despite our rows, and he could safely share me with any other. But as the business grew, caring for the horses became difficult, and as Himself got to know his tormentor better a sort of reciprocal spasmodic caring grew into a loyal friendship. But it was an as-and-when-you-please compliance, not an arrangement I could rely upon. I was not comfortable with the situation as complaints against That Horse and the time I spent away with him stacked up.

My chance for change came on one of those winter nights by the fire, and it came out of the blue. 'Freddie is going to get me more sheep.' No preambulations, no by-your-leave because you'll have to look after them when I'm at work, nothing like that.

'What?'

'We need more. The Board need you to keep certain numbers and anyway, it's ridiculous all that work for a few animals. There would be the same work with twice as many, or indeed more.'

Tell me about it! 'So sell them,' I belligerently suggested. 'And what Board needs me to keep more numbers?'

'The Board of Agriculture, of course.' The look was scathing. I had no interest in the intricacies of flock-keeping and was not admired for my attitude.

He then reiterated the oft-told tale of how tenanting land untouched by cloven hoof – with the emphasis on cloven – was not encouraged, and most importantly, there would be a reasonable profit to look forward to, and anyway, he liked sheep. I thought, I'm going to have to give in to this anyway, so I may as well get something out of it.

'OK, get your sheep. I'll look after the lot when you're away. No problem.' I was remembering how he encouraged me to double the size of the upstairs shower room with a 'no problem' attitude, and how all the problems that arose had put me forever off shifting walls. Maybe I could go along with this and put him forever off having sheep. 'No problem at all,' I assured him.

'No problem?' He sounded incredulous.

'None whatsoever. When you're away, I shall care for the sheep, look after the horses, do my bed and breakfast, care for our child and the cat, and any rabbit I may be getting, and anything else that comes my way. And all you have to do when you come home is look after your sheep and do the horses.'

'Oh, I could do for the horse all right – one of them, anyway!'

'You know what I mean; look after them. Properly.' Bronco was always under threat.

He looked at me. He has this way of looking, being a very handsome man, with those lovely blue eyes, crinkling at the corners when amused, and I saw that the deal was struck no matter what he said. And that was the way it was until it became untenable for both of us, his work on the rigs and mine in B&B becoming so demanding that it was impossible to run the sheep any longer. So my ruse worked, but it was a long time in coming.

But before this carefully-grown flock went, others came; this new lot of gimmers, two-year-olds ready for their first introduction to the joys of parenthood, from his shepherd friend who had a great eye for a breed. We looked at them in shock after Freddie departed, wondering at him as much as at the small, incredibly wild, scraggy-looking creatures our original handsome flock was investigating with disdainful superiority.

'Give them time,' the shepherd said before he left, and he was right. Next year they produced crackers of lambs that grew up to be as wild as themselves, whilst more of our extremely well-behaved flock reached the end of their lives, through one means or another. One was the dinner table, which came as a surprise to many of the guests.

Pet lambs were inevitable, and thankfully an exception to the cuisine of the house. Most were nurtured in the warmth of the kitchen, with a propensity to jump walls and visit whenever motivated.

Coping with cooking, serving and taking in new arrivals often did not allow full control of what was going on in the house. Heading for the dining room to check plates, the noise from a mere six guests sounded much too boisterous to blame exhibitionist horses or a playful cat.

I could not believe my eyes when I reached the dining room. There, standing staring at the company was Sister Kate, now a full-grown sheep, or a hog (hoggit) as we called the year-olds we kept from the previous lambing. We also called the ram a tup, which sounded much better when making reference to tupping time rather than ramming time! Gives the wrong impression, that. ('Is that sheep going to have a lamb?' my sister asked Neil when he was all of three and proudly pointing out one of our fat flock to his aunt. He looked at her with pure contempt. 'Don't be silly. The tup isn't out yet!' And indeed he was not, and well the child knew the drill; tupping first, lambing later.)

'What's a sheep doing in here?' I was accosted by an astonished diner, my own astonishment almost matching his. Sister Kate must have jumped a wall and ambled in through the open front door while I was in the kitchen.

'It's a she and she's looking for her brother!' I was quick to quip.

'Where's her brother gone then?'

'You're eating him.'

They weren't but they *were* eating mutton, though it was called by its much more marketable name, 'lamb'.

Sometimes the humour did not go down too well. Nor did the mutton on the menu. But that was the end result of the animals we killed – delicious, dark, tasty, thyme-flavoured mutton. They were hill sheep and to kill months-old lambs would have been ludicrous; they were too small and unflavoured. We usually had three year olds slaughtered, sometimes a little older. No guest would look at mutton on the menu but lamb, and especially Scottish Lamb, was the most precious commodity you could offer, even better than salmon, so of course our mutton was dressed as lamb. And they absolutely adored it, cooked as we were taught – traditionally slow, with considerable care, especially boiled, which made the best of Scotch broth.

During a meeting with the Prince of Wales – our Duke of Rothesay, his official title whilst in Scotland – he pontificated on the value of mutton and how he would like to see it better used. I could not agree with him more, but then, I'm totally prejudiced towards him. He's a genuinely lovely, warm-hearted man who knows a thing or two. His knowledge of the needs of this area drove him to set up an initiative in support of tourism – so vital to our economy – gaining him the admiration of the communities he so strongly supports.

Our mad flock became more difficult to govern, yet we never felt the need for a dog. Our first and last sheepdog had grown up close to the family when Neil was small and took great notions to his soft toys, one long-eared rabbit a firm favourite, which he would leap to rescue from the clothes rope when washed, and we in our ignorance thought it highly amusing. Experiencing his first lambing, the young collie dog took to tossing the lambs about in the way he did the toys and punctured the windpipe of one, causing dreadful upset to all, including the poor bereaved mother. He had to go and none took his place.

'You're my dog,' Himself would cheerfully announce as I hared this way and that to gather in the flock, muttering fiendish threats, aimed more at Himself than the flying sheep. The child became the pup in training but proved unreliable, though he learned, with his long-legged turn of speed, how to bring down a ewe with a flying tackle, a feat that did him proud in the Royal Marines, but once got him into serious trouble.

Sent out with his small recruit troupe on the moors to survive for days on one white rabbit, an idea that appalled me – and I don't know why he had to be so informative – because, yes, though they did debate the ethics of eating what they enjoyed petting, hunger overcame morality. With bunny gone and hunger growing, the knowledge that one recruit was a butcher in civil life, coupled with the fact that another reckoned he could catch a sheep single-handed, gave them the opportunity to dine high off the hoggit. The farmer made a fuss and they all landed in severe trouble.

We managed for years, running the flock and the horses between us. Lambing was like giving birth, remembered only for the good you got out of it, all the horrors forgotten as you looked forward to each April with growing anticipation and optimism, certain this year it would be perfect and I would get my black lamb. It never was, and I never did, but I was kept going with the promise that it would happen one year.

I didn't get a black lamb, but I did get a tartan one! What a boost to Scottish tourism he would have been. His mother went into lambing and was never like to produce, so I cornered her and had a go. I could make nothing of it and got Sanders from next door. It was as difficult a lambing as you could get but at the end we had the finest beast I ever saw emerge from a ewe. It was massive. What a head! Shoulders and back of a prize wrestler. And it was cream, red, brown, black and sparkling white. We had never seen anything like it. Sanders was a man who appreciated high standards and he admired this outstanding new arrival as the poor mother recovered.

'Could we breed from Tartan Tam?' I asked. I was warned not to name the lambs I fancied as it always ended in tears at sale time but when motivated by characteristics or colour, I christened with alacrity. Tartan Tam was as wild in nature as he was spectacular.

'Why not?' came the benign reply from any who would listen, and I looked forward with tremendous interest to this new breed I would call my own. I was fascinated. Himself's friend Freddie helped with docking the lambs to reduce the length of their tails and did the necessary to ensure no entire fully-productive tup emerged from the flock to upset the buyers. I explained how I wanted to keep Tartan Tam in pristine breeding condition as I was going to get lambs out of him as good looking as himself. All agreed he had wonderful breeding lines, as good as any seen for many a long year, and I set off to prepare a meal, delighted in this new interest I could take in the flock.

They had no hesitation in rendering him as useless as his brothers and I never forgave them the act of desecration, their excuse being you could never introduce that colouring into the flock. No one told me that. They just humoured me, so sod them and sod sheep as far as I was concerned.

They mollified me with assurances I was bound to get a black lamb. Logistics, statistics and the law of averages assured that after all those years with no black sheep in the flock other than myself, my time was close. And it was. They were right. I got one. But it was dead, after a long arduous labour, the only black lamb we ever had. 'Just be glad the ewe will be OK,' Colin MacKenzie tried to cheer me as I looked at the small jet-black body, lying still. It was a female, which, somehow, made it worse. I knew it was wrong to mentally barter the life of the lamb for the ewe, but I would have traded it.

I became thoroughly cheesed off with the whole caboodle. So they went, the whole lot, one fine day. I was having difficulty in hiding my delight, though Himself never held it against me, continuing to care for the horses during his leaves, the bond with Bronco growing year on year, with a total capitulation and acceptance of the expenses of attending shows, tearing about the country when I should be here working, and all the time and costs of grooming, shoeing and veterinary necessities. But I began to realise that time was running out for horse activities, our equines spending more of their summers semi-retired while I gave more and more time to my growing business and my interest in what exact product the tourism industry in the area was marketing to the world.

Then, trading lambs on the hoof hit the sky, with prices we could only have dreamed of, coinciding with a long spell of unemployment for the man Himself. The decision was made to get sheep back on the croft. It was mutual, born of a weird longing for something that had gone out of our lives which looking back we thought had been good. It was not, but we deluded ourselves in the desire to put cash back into the depleted coffers, and onto the croft came a dozen ladies.

Oh, yes, they were ladies, and ladies of distinction.

Their proud owner delivered them by sheep-box trailer, and, as each trotted down the ramp, they stood by him, to get their heads rubbed and petted, all the time receiving assurances that they were going to a good home. They were spotless, perfectly formed and all very like each other, probably because they were related. They were obviously devoted to each other, and each was in lamb. They were also beautifully behaved. We had a lot of ground for them to roam and with great dignity they made immediate friends with the horses – one becoming so close to Bronco he would invite her into his loose-box, an unheard of condescension. The new ewes seemed happy with us and we were delighted with them.

The first of the big renovations on the house was under way and I had an extremely busy season ahead, the money needed as Himself stayed worryingly out of work. The oil sector could be like that, with jobs on the rigs at a premium. Then, as winter turned to a dirty, wet and snowy spring, he was offered a job on a rig and grabbed it. We celebrated this fortune, I encouraging anything that would allow us a bank balance again.

'What about those sheep in lamb?'

'No problem!' And I meant it. I had to cope.

By this time the work in the house had grown considerably. I now had five rooms and Taste of Scotland dinners to serve. My friend Barbara worked with me each morning from Monday to Friday, leaving me to the dinners and the weekend work myself. It was a routine that suited us both and my wonderful new facilities added joy to the pressures growing all around me. I felt invincible. Barbara and I got on like a house on fire. You could have searched the world and not found a person more capable of keeping house, and her reliability was beyond reproach. Our laughter filled the house, rarely alleviated by any kind of spat. I would be fine, I assured Himself as he took off, convinced the first lamb would arrive before he returned.

'There's only 12, for goodness sakes. I've coped with dozens!'

I think he must have had a premonition. He was a realist, he insisted, not a pessimist as I insisted. But I was my usual optimistic self.

When I walked round the field in the early evening, one of the ladies followed me all the way. She stood at the gate below the road, looking towards the house until I made my next round after dinner was served. She followed me again with an increasingly pathetic look on her face. Before darkness, she actually looked sick and I began to worry.

I went out long before dawn next morning and she was still on her feet, but this time the rest of the flock had gathered round her. They were not happy. By torchlight I noticed a small discharge from her rear end. She was going to lamb. It would be fine. She looked faintly huffed when I left her and did not return for a couple of hours, though I brought food for all. There was little change in their stance and the offer of food was spurned, by all. That was worrying, so I ran to Barbara's – she was always up at the crack of dawn – and asked if her husband, Uisdean, would have a look.

Eventually it dawned on us he would have to lamb her, which he did. The lamb was perfect, as was the second, which should have been easy for her to produce but which also had to be taken from her. She was delighted with them both. Her friends admired approvingly then left for their food. All was in order.

Eleven out of the 12 gave birth to twins, excellent lambs,

and the single was a cracker. But not one lambed herself, every one demanding assistance. They allowed me to lamb if Uisdean was not about, and they were not difficult lambings. It appeared to me as if the ladies were too posh to push! I only saw them once behave in a less than dignified manner and that was when Willie Robert, their original owner, stopped by the roadside one day, got out of his car and gave what sounded like a coded call. Up the field they raced, tails circling wildly as feet flew, baaing and careering to the fence like hooligans. Despite not seeing him for a couple of years, their welcome was almost overwhelming. It was quite heartwarming to behold.

High entertainment began for the guests that first mad spring I was left to do the lambing. Life took wing, from morning to night. The mornings were bad enough, but the nights? They were something else.

The programme went like this:

The refusal to lamb without assistance was new to me and demanded so much of my time I was thankful it was early in the season. But we did have guests most nights and by the time half the sheep – forgive me, 'ladies' – had birthed, I was well into serving a houseful of guests. I took the few yet to lamb up to the fields close to the house, so I could keep an eye on them. When one showed signs she might just want her lamb produced, I moved her with a companion into the field in front of the house, depriving the horses of their nightly performance. One night in particular was very wet and dreich.

Preparations for dinner were made in the usual way and I dressed as always in high heels, my favourite style of shoe; a tight skirt, which was in vogue and probably the only type I owned; and a decent blouse or shirt. With a sheep in the front park, my eye was as much on the window as on the table. About halfway through serving the soup, down went my sheep and gave a light-hearted heave. I was on full alert now but not too worried. Her companion still grazed.

Then she slipped down the brae so I could not see what was going on at the action end. 'Blast it!'

Quickly, shoes off, skirt dumped, jeans and boots on. Grab a jacket and woolly hat and out the back door, flying through the first gate, round the corner and into the field. A sideways glance towards the house showed a guest's head idly turned towards the window, but the transformation of gear would hide my identity. As far as the guests were concerned their hostess was in the kitchen, seeing to their dinner, and a farm-hand was attending an animal. Nothing very interesting there.

Madam was having me on. Nothing doing as yet. 'Keep an eye on her,' I appealed to her companion as I rushed off.

Back in, gear off, hands washed, mud splashes wiped off face and the next course under way. This only when it ran smoothly – times of interrupting telephone calls giving rise to hurried shouts of, 'I'm lambing,' and slamming down the receiver are not worth recounting; nor are the urgent dives to answer the impatient ringing of the doorbell wearing only my knickers as I desperately try to get the skirt over my head, being just too distressing to relate.

I had a huge kitchen now and I made use of every available space as I dumped used crockery and pans everywhere, my sole concentration being on getting a perfect main course into the hostess and ready to serve.

Calmly into the dining room, not a hair out of place, picking up the empty soup plates, making idle conversation, giving the impression I didn't have a care in the world. As if. A sideways glance and the bloody animal was on her back! Quickly smiling at the two talkers who had yet to finish, I announced, all charm, 'Take your time. You're on holiday,' big smile, 'with all the time in the world.'

Aaaahhhhh! Shoes off, skirt off, boots on and away. Grab hat though. I had very long dark hair and though tied back, it had to be kept under a hat – I still hoped the guests knew nothing of what was going on. Hell! Trousers! The fashion was wide-legged flares so no problem as jeans easily pull on, then into the field, panting hard. You would think it was me about to give birth! My casualty's companion now took a critical stance by her side. If she'd had eyebrows, she would have raised them in contempt. I eased her off her back, but there was no sign of a nose being presented yet. She looked at me with marble-striped accusing eyes. Her help-mate looked at me and bleated plaintively. It added to my anxiety.

'Look, why don't you just get bloody on with it instead of making a spectacle of yourself?'

Her hard stare implied it was not she who was making the spectacle of herself. Racing back, boots kicked off before I reached the house, hat already flung by the greenhouse and trousers dropped at the back door, hands washed as I passed the loo, skirt on and shoes missing! No time to think. Hair plastered onto head from the hat and the rain, wide smile plastered onto face from necessity. Back into dining room and graciously lifting two plates, long empty. On the way out I tripped over my shoes, left abandoned in the hallway. Recovering, I spied my face in the mirror, with two large mud splashes up the left side. Very becoming! They probably thought it was gravy.

Mud removed and shoes back on, the main course was served with commendable dignity and I relaxed. They would take their time. I made sure they had everything required as I glanced out the window. Herself, my lambing lady, was nowhere to be seen, but her mate stood there with an anxious look on her face. There was a slight incline in the park and the missing ewe must have been out of sight on the other side of a dip. What a curse. Back out of and into the appropriate gear, donning the wet trousers and boots where dumped. Oh, yuck! What madness had brought my life to this?

Hearing me coming, my sheep rose and made her way back

to the horses' favourite performing area right in front of the dining room window, which was not where I wanted her. I had time now and wanted to investigate her condition, but she was on her feet and they were big sheep and I was not good at couping them under the best circumstances. I had to get her down.

She began to lose her ladylike demeanour and fought back at my every attempt to bring her down, the tussle seeing me brought down several times before I looked up to see we had an appreciative audience in the window, and two inquisitive horses leaning over the gate. The watchful accomplice stood well off but was bleating loudly, adding to my wretchedness. Well, hat gone, lying in the mud, the guests were bound to know it was me now. Nevertheless, I wished they would go back to their food. I was miffed they would let all my efforts under duress get cold, but no doubt such entertainment was rarely theirs and was too good to miss.

An almighty effort brought my ewe to the ground, and being tame and lazy – too darned lazy to lamb herself – which could not be taken for granted anyway, the possibility of complications ensuring my attention – she lay there and I could easily see the two tiny black hooves with the little nose all properly presented, ready to be pushed into the world. I calculated all I yet had to do for the table: plates to clear, puddings to dish up, sweets to serve, cheese board to offer and coffee to set up. Could I leave her?

Uisdean and Barbara were not on the telephone so did not know my predicament and in the time it would take them to get there, I could do the job myself, as I had done now on several occasions with this lot of prima donnas, so I dismissed the idea of getting help.

Besides, I had this audience, coming and going from window to table, and producing a lamb would give a reason for my irrational behaviour. Firmly gripping the feet, I gave a long, hard, steady pull and out popped the lamb. It snuffled and snorted and shook its beautiful head, ears all floppy and wet. Round to the head of the mother I placed this newborn miracle, and she accepted it with soft mutterings and many nuzzlings. What a relief; she could just as easily have said it's not mine, you have it, and then I would really have been in trouble. This happened all too often and meant either forcing the mother to allow the lamb to get the precious cholesterol, or taking it off her and feeding it down the lamb's throat by tube or bottle. Worse, the mother might want the lamb but the lamb refuse to suck. There were no end of computations in my mind as I placed the newborn in front of the mother. What if she had no milk? Then it would be back to the house to make up the precious feed, a sticky horrid job, not easily carried out in a kitchen where every spare space hosted the remnants of a four-course dinner for ten. I patted her head in relief as all appeared to be well, told her what a fine mother she was, what a beautiful child she had, and raced off back to the house.

The same quick-change routine, but less hurried as I had lost steam and knew I had more time now to prepare desserts and everything else. The kitchen was growing in chaos as plates were taken from the dining room, to choruses of delight at the sight of seeing a sheep lambed, and by me of all people. Imagine that! It caused no end of interest and quizzical looks.

'Do you do this kind of thing often?' from amused guest.

'Only when in season!' from cheeky but euphoric hostess.

By the time the hot pudding and cold sweets were served, milady in the field had her lamb suckling, little curly tail wiggling in delight, the sign of a hungry belly being satisfyingly filled. I was high on success. The house always had a happy atmosphere but now it buzzed with the excitement of new life. The guests asked their inevitable questions and I answered with pleasure. When I came in with the cheese board the new mother was down again and giving another heave. Could I leave her alone? Was she safe? Would she lamb this one herself? Oh, surely she would.

I started setting up the coffee table in the lounge with the huge picture window, which showed the troublesome evil creature was on her back again. There was absolutely no need for this at all. The wee lamb was staggering about and I could easily see the front feet of the next one preparing for the world. But I had to get closer to check the nose lay on the feet, otherwise there was trouble.

This time I made no pretence. I shouted, 'I'm off! I'll be back!' and got the offer of help from more than one voice. They were female voices:

'Darling, you go and help. He is so good in emergencies, just run along dear. Mrs Campbell, would you just pop his pudding back into the oven?'

'Yes, James will go too. Mrs Campbell, would you put James's sweet back in the fridge, or shall I do it?' Oh, yes, I have all the time in the world to be faffing about putting puddings and sweets in ovens and fridges, and the last thing I needed was one of them, from their genteel backgrounds, in the chaotic unbelievable debris of my kitchen, which was piled up on the worktops and most of the floor.

Help from a guest, unless a fully-fledged shepherd – and we had one of these too, one half of the Bells, who joined our June house party for about 20 years, as well as making lambing-time visits – was the last thing I needed, but by the time I was ready, out they trooped in their posh clothes and expensive shoes. It was the last thing the spoilt patient needed, too. One look at them and off she took, back end protruding with the desire to be born, galloping round the park like a heathen. She did not like strangers, as few sheep do when lambing, so I could hardly blame her, but I sure felt like blaming the obtrusive and unhelpful guests. They just wanted to satisfy curiosity and help was not on their agenda. At my request to corner the wildly careering animal they looked sheepishly at their feet and said they would have to get more adequate footwear. Did I have wellingtons in their size? Oh, yes, sir, let me fetch you a pair and we'll try them on to see if they suit. No problem at all. What colour would you like? I'll see to your request while the patient does herself a massive injury. All in a day's work!

My look said it all, and they went. The alarmed mother calmed down, another lamb was taken from her, and all three seemed stable as I raced back to the house. All signs of angst gone, I got the guests settled round the coffee table in the lounge, two sharing the window seat so they could enjoy the tableau of nursing mother, concerned aunt and admiring horses. The rain had eased and there was still a glow of light, it being early May. I was just beginning to think I had it licked, hoping no other ewe would lamb tonight so I could get the place sorted out by midnight. Then I did a double take. For goodness sakes! The concerned aunt had lambed, all by herself. In half an hour, no fuss, it had just popped out and was up on its feet, all cleaned, new mother nudging encouragement to suckle.

'Oh, how wonderful. Isn't nature to be admired? A new lamb almost as we turned our back to pick up our coffee. They say if you leave them alone they make no fuss and just produce their lambs without interference,' with a very meaningful look in my direction, from the helpful James's wife.

Oh, I could be gullible, but it was usually people who pulled the wool over my eyes, not animals. That may be the way it should be, but not with this lot. Something was not right. Back into the dirty, wet, yucky attire, smiles replaced with a weary sigh.

The new mother had given her second lamb to the watch-ful aunt, who was delighted to get one without all that huffing and puffing and downright ineptitude from these new owners, who obviously didn't have a clue how to treat ladies of their breeding. This was a huge problem. A thief in the flock: ewes who went round trying to steal the firstborn from new mothers when they were busy attending to a twin. They were very determined and many a row erupted in the fields when the new mother cottoned on to the deception before the crofter did.

It took time and effort to separate them. I left the extremely annoyed aunt in the park with the horses while I made for the barn, the mother following my distressed bleating as I mocked the lamb I carried in one arm, surprisingly heavy and hard on the back. I scooped the other to my chest, going backwards so as to assure the mother that I had her precious bundles and she would have them back if she just followed. My bleating calls were charged with genuine distress, which made them very real for the sheep to follow. The lambs were silent in their contented awe of this new world they had been pulled into. By now they must have wondered who exactly would be mothering them.

A glance at the dining-room window showed no excited faces peering out, the attention span of visitors being rather fleeting. They have time only to get a taste of your travails, but they do love to know how you live your life in this far off area, as remote as it is beautiful, and their interest comes from a genuine desire to absorb the atmosphere of a community, which should be encouraged – but maybe not in the ways I was obliged to at times!

A straw bed was always ready for emergencies but my fear was that having willingly given her friend her second-born, the mother would not now accept it back. If there were complications, I was going to get them; but no, she took them both, and in exhausted relief I totally forgave her all her histrionics.

Then came the mad dash back to change from a shattered but triumphant crofter into the svelte and entertaining hostess, whom you would never guess would spend the next hours cleaning up the wreck of a kitchen, between trips to the barn and round the fields to ensure the rest of the ladies were preparing for an unbroken night's sleep.

'Any more lambs yet?' This was always the first question during lambing time, taking over from, 'Have you people in?'

Weather conditions were the second topic, especially when it was sunny and warm and delightful. 'It won't last,' could be relied upon from the morose older crofters.

'Yes, got a couple of beauties last night,' I crowed at the Post Office the next morning. My highly delighted guests had already left, eager to tell their next hosts how they fared on a croft in Melvich.

'Did everything go OK?'

'Of course! No problems, no problems at all.'

7

Bums in Beds

THE ADVENT OF A new body to help put the fledgling tourism industry on the map at the tail end of the '60s was met with little interest in its initial stages, from the established B&Bs at any rate. Then it began to dawn on some: this Scottish Tourist Board was setting up offices in just about every locality and those offices existed solely for the purpose of enticing visitors inside to seek information and, much more interesting, beds for the night. The situation that grew from this innovative method of meeting visitors' needs put much power in the hands of the Tourist Board employees behind the desks; power which went to many heads.

I was blind to its influence when I joined, and to the fact that those women – the majority of those who took on what was poorly-paid part-time work being female – had the opportunity to serve friends and cock a snook at enemies. Those Tourist Information Centre employees met many challenges, their job not being easy. Some delighted in the chance to help operators they saw as friends, whilst others were scrupulously fair in their dealings with the tourists and the operators, be they friend or foe.

The problem appeared to lie in allocating the bums to the beds. In time, the arrival of the mobile phone clawed the feet from under the lot of them, giving autonomy to the bums to find their own beds without recourse to a TIC person. Today the set-up in the TIC establishments has become totally unrecognisable from those early days, yet tales still abound of foibles and frolics and unmitigated dissatisfaction. But the real power lay, as it still does – though not to such a high degree – with the inspectors. Wow, did they cause consternation in their 20-year journey from the Tourist Board inspectors of back then through to the VisitScotland advisor we have today.

Inspectors were born of the need to grade quality when the STB Quality and Standards Scheme was initiated. More and more homes were seeing the value of taking in paying guests to add to their income. The old Highlands and Islands Development Board encouraged new businesses in this direction, with grants to aid the building of new homes intended to be part of this sector, as well as to provide better and better facilities for established operators.

This was good for the growth of the Highlands but for many a long year little was done to teach marketing skills to people who were often running their first business. Scotland was a popular domestic destination, with a growing foreign market that added considerably to the chances of filling beds in those busy middle months of the season, but as always there was a downside. The influx of visitors generated by Tourist Board marketing exacerbated the inability to provide beds for every traveller roaming the highways and byways during peak season, whilst the lack of business in the then shoulder months meant a scrabble for the few available bums on offer in April and a glut in August. This was before fleets of mobile homes began to travel the country in convoys, seeking roadside parking for the night instead of beds in the local B&Bs, giving proprietors further anxiety when trying to fill beds.

Something had to be done, and this became the remit of the

Scottish Tourist Board, initially under the umbrella of the HIDB
in the Highland area, soundly supported by the then Scottish
Office. How the spread of visitors could be handled was a
mystery to most toiling at the coal face, though elucidation
would come via the offer of membership in the different local
area boards of the STB.

Thus began the seasonal sport of counting cars.

'You had people last night!' Nose twitching without a modicum of congratulations, the voice of suspicion snapping from
this particular B&B owner's pursed lips.

'Me? No, never saw a soul for days.' An honest and cheery
answer which earned me a look of reproof reinforced with a sniff.

'But you had a car!' A note of rebuke creeping into the
quizzical voice. Couldn't deny that. I still had friends, and
occasionally one called.

There were children whose little white faces could be seen
pressed against the window panes of the school bus, leaving
you to believe their objective was to note the cars and report
back later. It was highly amusing to someone with a sense of
humour as trigger-happy as mine. They could just as easily
have asked my son, who boarded the bus. He would have
informed, no bother. It was only me he kept in the dark as he
entered his teenage years, going about his business with a
furtive look over his shoulder to see just how much I gleaned
of his comings and goings. He thought it highly funny and
would never have dreamed of telling me who had, or who had
not, got cars. Asking would have been futile. He couldn't have
cared less; even his forays into lining his own pocket could not
elicit an interest.

Then there was a genuine friend who had no axe to grind,
no longer doing B&B herself, but she liked to know what was
what. 'You had people in last night!'

'No. What makes you think that?' There hadn't even been
a car near the place.

I got the look again. 'You must have had people. You had sheets on the line.'

'Those were our own sheets.' Said without rancour, hearing the same statement throughout the season. Surely the watching public were aware there were times when I just had to wash our own linen; hers was never off the line, she being an ardent washer of anything that smacked of a day's use. Despite being close friends, the look implied I was hiding things, but it amused me too much for me to become weary of it.

I took it as a communal interest in my well-being, even when someone was hell bent on determining what went on under my roof, using the guise of a so-called friendship, making sure she knew every nook and cranny of our home, then forever accosting me on the telephone, literally shrieking, 'You had four cars outside your house last night!' The voice was so intoned with accusation, I felt obliged to explain what was entirely my own business.

'I know. One of them was our own!' Exasperation gave rise to sarcasm, for this inquisition about cars was getting out of hand. Himself said I was a sap when I did not reply, 'It's none of your frigging business woman,' but I was a great believer in keeping the peace. In fact, I intensely disliked confrontation, which seemed so unnecessary, live and let live being much closer to my heart.

Not to be put off, her answer was as sharp as it was swift, 'Four as well as your own!' She could count.

And like an idiot I would explain, for the sake of that peace: 'My sister was here for the weekend,' which she often was. It was easier to give away your own business than to have the angst. Eventually, as ever, something would happen once too often, and, for the sake of your sanity, you'd adopt a 'you go your way and I'll go mine' attitude, and wish you had done so years before.

What gave a little credence to the policing of cars by an

operator was the need for establishments that operated, as we did for several years, with more than three letting bedrooms to pay commercial rates instead of council tax. We were one of the first B&Bs in Scotland who were asked to make the change, back when commercial rates were not subsidised. By the time the rates and the council tax were reasonably similar, we had cut our rooms back to three, with only six letting spaces. We kept our fire certification, but changed our insurance policy to one allowing for accommodating six paying guests, that being a great boost to small B&Bs. Often I got enquiries about the legislation when new operators came into being or established B&Bs changed their circumstances. It could be a minefield.

Additionally, once you became a member of the STB and bought into their literature to grow your business, you had to state the number of rooms you offered for guest accommodation, paying a very tiny sum per room in addition to the cost of your advert. Was my inquisitor concerned that we had the audacity to put into operation one more room than we had paid for, doing the Tourist Board out of what was then a matter of pence per annum? No, the car-counting wifie was not taking a tally in protection of Tourist Board revenue, but in the belief that you should only fill your beds with bums when she had first filled hers! It was a strange and insular attitude not known to me in the initial years, when I worked happily with the women of the area. But times, they were a-changin'.

Himself knew little of the missiles hurled in my direction or the tears shed in the quiet of the night. Eventually, driven by the distress of it all and the opportunity to go in a different direction, I seriously contemplated giving it all up. After one outrageous ploy to keep people away from my beds – and there were many – I went to sleep vowing I would take the office job on offer. But, in an overnight conversion, I began to dream those dreams, got up in the morning enthused with a steely determination to continue and, instead of knuckling under the pressure, I upped the game entirely, surpassing all my own expectations of what could be achieved, not only in my own business but out there in the thick of the delivery of the tourism product to Scotland.

I discovered, too, that favours come in many guises. Way into the future, when facing the long and weary fight with cancer, an unexpected but hard kick came from the same direction. It was my reaction to this unbelievable method of removing a player from the field that drove me to accept the invitation onto the board of management of the local enterprise company, the first of many such invitations and nominations, changing forever the route my life had taken. It was a change I regretted only in that it depleted my attention to everything but the needs of the boards I served on and the requirements of my guests, leaving little time for family and friends, and no social life whatsoever, and leading me to abandon my guitar along with my horses.

Counteracting this harshness, the warmth and encouragement from the community itself, as well as from friends and family, during my fight with cancer just had to be met with the most positive of attitudes. Bless them all for their goodness, natural to them and easy to understand when you grow up and live amongst such people. It's what you expect, get in abundance and try to dish out, making it difficult at times to accept the opposite.

8

A Room with a View

ONE QUESTION WE ARE constantly asked is, 'Do you have a favourite guest?' The answer is simple, but not the answer that is expected. It is not a specific person, because that would be impossible; we get so many genuinely lovely people. We get the opposite too, but they are few and far between; their effect would surely drive you out of the business should they inveigle themselves into your establishment more than once in a very blue moon.

A dear friend of mine ran an excellent B&B for years, until she came across one such couple, who had left a trail of misery across Scotland. My friend had the courage to call in the police to put a stop to their practice of walking out of accommodations after staying for days and not paying. Their revenge upon her home while waiting for an officer of the law to arrive forced her to burn her entire bedding, mattress and all, and led to a sad rethink of the business she was in. Having been in that business for much, much longer, I pleaded with her not to let a couple of ignoramuses destroy the pleasure she undoubtedly had in her work, but to no avail. The fact that this can actually happen, yet that it happens so very, very seldom – not the attempt to get free board but the disgusting repercussions – proves how good the vast majority of the travelling public is.

My favourite person would have to be not just challenged in the follicle department but totally bereft of any hirsute tendencies. Unfortunately, this rules out the much-loved Italians, and it gives the Swedes a higher rating, for next best thing to being completely bald is being blonde; even out of a bottle will do, provided the roots have been newly treated.

Chasing the elusive hair is one of the most frustrating and demanding jobs you can do. Everything else pales in significance. There is absolutely nothing worse than finding the bodily remains of a previous occupant in your bedroom when you arrive, even if everything else is sparkling. You book into a five-star establishment knowing it must achieve 100% in housekeeping in order to retain that status. But that hair can elude like no other unwanted particle.

I leave an en suite spick and span, certain there is not a hair in sight when I close the door with satisfaction, knowing a job well done. Something takes me back, and there, defying all logic, is the hair. It is usually black. What worries me is, what about the blond hairs? Does one take out spectacles and get down on hands and knees yet again, to ensure they have not made their magic reappearance all over the place?

Attending a posh dinner, I noticed a very glamorous friend at the top table, looking her usual stunning self. She had just started a super new job after working at a local B&B for a while and I hastened to congratulate her when we adjourned after dinner. Crossing her long elegant legs and flicking an unseen speck from her little black dress, she raised an eyebrow, 'It'll sure beat cleaning other people's short and curlies out of the shower trays.'

That set the tone on the rest of our conversation, interspersed with much hilarity.

'It's not the short and curlies that get me, but the long and sleek ones. I find them far harder to remove...' but we were interrupted by a suave, very bald gentleman, bearing down on us with a glint in his eye.

'Now, what are you two lovely ladies talking about?' He was gallant enough to be inclusive in his remark but the glint was not beamed in my direction. I had no hesitation in answering, 'The type of person we would most like to have in the bedroom.'

He lasciviously leaned towards us, 'And where would I come into that category?'

'On first appearance, a front runner, but a closer inspection would be necessary.' Our laughter drew others into the company and, fortunately, the conversation moved to higher ground.

But to get back to that special person, our favourite guest. After ascertaining the need for complete baldness, there is a very serious second necessity. This person must be a graduate of the school of thought that connects the tongue to the brain, allowing for some kind of synergy between enthusiastic declarations of appreciation and actual behaviour.

You can be so easily lulled into delighting in your guests' demeanour when you show them into their bedroom and they wax lyrical about the view, having been very specific in their booking requirement that only a room with that view would suffice. They then delight in the amenities of the room when you show that not only is there an adequate wardrobe but a cupboard, in which they can store any large cases, bits and pieces, anything they want out of their way.

'How wonderful. May we keep our golf clubs in here?'

'Of course you can, that's what it's there for – whatever you want to keep out of your way, and it easily takes the fully-extended case stand.' Which will keep the case out of my way too, I blissfully thought as I smiled and offered tea and home bakes in the lounge when they were ready.

Relaxing in the lounge, taking a serious look at the breakfast menu while they sipped their tea and eyed up the home-made shortbread, my guests, having had time to properly peruse their room, told me how much they appreciated the attention to detail, a favourite comment, describing how they enjoyed following *Scotland's Best B&Bs*, which so often gave this extremely high standard of cleanliness and these little touches that impress so much.

'That's a super couple,' I enthused as I returned to the kitchen. 'It's lovely to have people who appreciate everything and say so. It will be great looking after them. Isn't it good they've booked in for nearly a week.'

Oh boy! What a surprise lay in wait for my unsuspecting eyes.

Next morning, sun shining bright, I went into the bedroom after they had taken off for the day, still drowning in bon-homie and enthusiasm for all there was on offer. I was greeted with windows closely curtained and the blind pulled down to its fullest extent. So much for enjoying the view, a view so absolutely stunning on a sunny morning, the blue from the bay contrasting with the beginnings of purple on the cliff tops, sloping into the gentle greenery of fields bordered by grey stone dykes and spotted with clusters of creamy-coloured sheep. The yellowing marram grass can be seen, fringing the sands that etch out the salmon river, the Halladale, flowing towards that big beautiful bay. Into this curve lies the horseshoe shape of Bighouse Lodge and its walled gardens, close to the mouth of the river, but far enough away to make its own statement. It is a view many say has not been bettered on their entire holiday.

Philistines, I thought, as I drew up the blind, revealing a picture many would die for. And their first priority had been a room with a view!

That was only the beginning. Getting to the window to let light and air into the room proved a bit of an assault course. Picking my way over one very large suitcase abandoned on the floor, I pulled open the storage cupboard. There the golf bag resided in solitary splendour, surrounded by lots of space and two wooden case racks, neatly stacked against the wall. So much for the store cupboard that was pounced upon in the preview of the room!

I did not interfere with the bags dumped here and there. Clothing was heaped on chairs, with papers strewn on every available surface, yet the wardrobe lay empty. Various shoes were encased in the bedspread, made-to-measure by the most expensive firm in the north and costing more than twice what they would be paying for the room for the week, now twisted into an unrecognisable heap and dumped on the floor.

I moved towards the upheaval that was the bed. I much prefer an upheaval because at least then I know I must remake the bed, instead of having to wonder if the half-made effort that greets me is my guests' preferred method for comfort. This is always a puzzle, especially when the bed appears reasonably well made, but has enough of a crumpled effect to be suspicious. The pillows are well-enough plumped, the sheet neatly turned over the duvet and the bedcover smoothed out over the lot, but something alerts me, some instinct tells me that all is not as well as it looks. The quickest and best tip for getting to the bottom of whether or not to interfere is to haul back the cover at the foot of the bed and lift the duvet, and there you will find either a crumpled mess of screwed-up sheets that demands a remake, or a neatly-smoothed-out bottom sheet, with the top sheet well turned down over the lot. Then you know this thoughtful guest made a serious job here and should just be thankful for small mercies. And be thankful too there is no leering red nail lying in wait. These things happen, you'll be shocked to discover as you read on!

Speaking of making up beds, I was exceedingly fortunate when I went into this line as a rank amateur to have two sisters who were willing to show me some of the ropes. As to the beds, it was blankets and quilts with light covers in those days, and my older sister, Sandra, who had started training as a nurse before deciding on a career change, took charge of the bed-making and showed me hospital corners and how to bounce a coin off the blankets. It was good to see how a bottom sheet should be stretched to a comfortable smoothness that would remain for the duration of the night, but I instinctively adhered to the belief that beds and nests had something in common. Tight cornering that left room for only a coin to bounce was not my idea of meeting requirements. There's not much fun in bouncing coins when an inviting bed can hold so many other possibilities.

My beds, to my great delight, are commented on daily, for their extreme comfort and their ability to lull the occupant into a great night's sleep. I tell them I impregnate the pillows with a sprinkling of kelpie dust to ensure pleasant dreams. I then have to explain the origins of a kelpie as they seriously consider buying this effective herb, admitting it is a Highland faerie, a water nymph, and is better left to its own devices due to a per-verse streak worse than even I could be driven to. Immediate note is taken, and a little scepticism enters into their view of my *savoir-vivre*. A five-star rating often implies no sense of humour is to be found on the premises, but fortunately for me this is not a requirement.

The first thing I do when I stay at a hotel is strip the bed and remove the yards of sheet tucked under the mattress. Often a mere inch turns over the scabby blanket you are at times met with, so that the sheet only comes up to your armpit. Where, oh where did these people learn to make beds? It seems to be universal among hotels, regardless of rating, unless you are fortunate enough to get a duvet; but then you seldom get a top sheet, which I prefer. Where did the belief come from that sheets are meant to be under the mattress, with a mean turn-down of an inch? This is certainly not the way beds were made by the housemaids of days gone by, trained on the premises by women whose status in the community was governed by the pride they took in their work. Like hospital matrons, the reintroduction of such capable females into the hospitality industry would do more to satisfy customers than the style of training often on offer, reliant more upon college courses and achieving bits of paper rather than hands-on ability to do the job.

I follow Sandra's advice and do an excellent 'Department of Health' bottom sheet, then I make sure the top sheet is laid with a turn-down over the duvet of at least two-to-three feet. The bottom of the sheet is loosely tucked in, leaving room for a bit of scrabbling about and not imprisoning the feet, just in case a little merriment necessitating movement is on the agenda that night. How I wish I could remember the name of the very elderly gentleman from the American South who asked for a bed with a footboard.

'I'm sorry, all our beds have headboards. We have nothing with a footboard.' I was very regretful.

'Oh, I suppose we'll just have to make do.' His face reflected his disappointment, a hangdog expression lingering as he went on, 'But at my age, dear lady, you need a bit of purchase.' It took me a minute to work it out, but I got there.

The temptation to tell colleagues that 'Purchase Facilities' is a new criterion on the QA requirement lists is rather strong. Can you imagine the reaction when next I sit down as a member on the committee of VisitScotland overseeing the Quality and Standards Scheme, discussing the discriminatory aspect of the Disability Act, if I were to say 'Don't you think we should be adding to the list, "footboards on beds" so that elderly guests might have the added assistance of purchase?'

Nowadays, with footboards becoming fashionable again, we are more likely to be asked for a bed without one so that six-foot-four Nordic chaps are not restricted by the standard length.

Pillows too can be a make-or-break factor, and who can blame those who travel with their own? We place two pillows, each of a different type, for every guest, and have two more at hand, along with the extra blanket that is requisite in quality-assured establishments. When this is pointed out in the guidance tour of the rooms, the guest nearly always says, 'Goodness, we won't need an extra blanket here,' but many like to change the duvet for a blanket and having a top sheet and a spare blanket gives this option.

My younger sister Muriel also offered her help when I was starting out. She was then single and spent a lot of time with me when Himself was working away. When she came to stay I proudly showed her the table I had set up for high tea. I thought it lovely.

Her howls of laughter puzzled more than offended. It was a nice cloth and the china was bone, gifted by herself as a wedding present. I stepped back with arms folded across my chest ready for battle. 'OK, then. What's wrong with it?' The belligerence in my voice was barely disguised.

She had been trained as a waitress in the days when training actually meant time spent at a hotel school, followed by years working under head waiters, before you dared consider yourself fit to be let loose, unsupervised, on the public. With a few deft movements she altered the entire look of the table, without adding or subtracting an article. It was like magic.

'I don't believe that,' I said, grinning at her. She had moved all the condiments into a single group close to the middle, pre-serving centre stage for a tier of the cakes, scones, pancakes and breads traditionally served with high teas. She then picked up the milk jug and placed it neatly to one side along with the sugar bowl, laying the sugar spoon between jug and bowl. The jams she set on the opposite side of the table alongside the butter, with butter knife and jam spoons placed between, and then started on the china and cutlery.

She turned the cup over in the saucer, giggling, 'People like to check the make of your china, and doing it this way avoids the disaster when some smart alec turns the cup upside down after putting the milk in it! You'd be surprised how often I've seen that happening.'

She then picked up the side knife from the side plate, replacing it with a nicely-shaped napkin. The knife she set on the outside of the larger meat knife, ensuring the cutting edges of both faced towards the place mats, and lined up the fork on the opposite side, with the teaspoon on the right of the smaller knife.

She smothered another snigger as she picked up the mats for the tea and water jug from their separate locations and placed them side by side at a position convenient to the guest. She may have done more and, I have no doubt, laughed more, but the set-up is still what I use today for breakfasts, with various additions that time has brought about. Like the goujons of herring suggested by one on-the-ball advisor, I get plaudits that should go to her for a fine table.

When travelling, it is only occasionally that I sit at a table set in the haphazard ways of my youth, and the temptation to do a Muriel on it is almost overwhelming.

9

Taken Out by the SAS

A CASUAL ENQUIRY, 'How's it going, Connie?', at times would elicit a curt reply, accompanied by eyes raised to the heavens, 'You don't want to know.' This happened after the farewell of either a particularly hairy person or a very posh person, the latter necessitating further comment as I swung through the fire door to help: 'You are now entering into a danger zone,' she would warn with nose firmly pinched as she headed for a bedroom.

At times, the posher the accent, the pooier the loo left to be made pristine for the next guest. 'Very posh, that pair,' I would comment upon new arrivals, getting the invariable reply, 'Not too posh to poo, though!'

The stinky loos are salutary reminders when you meet those people who look down their noses at you while boasting of the wonderful accommodation they offer their visitors and the superior lifestyle they lead. It's usually done in such a manner that you're left in no doubt that you just don't measure up. Don't fall into the trap of defending your own standards, just smile beguilingly and say, 'Such fun, isn't it? All that loo cleaning and mucking out of showers.' And if they raise their brows and answer, 'We have staff,' just stand on their toes as you exit their company, as Bronco would advise.

'How's it going, Connie?' drew various replies, all preceded with, 'You don't want to know!' Given the bald statement with no further elucidation, I kept well out of it, but on occasion there was a head-tilting pause followed by one of Connie's inventive suggestions.

'I don't know what was going on in there last night but I would suggest to you that it would be more like you to be sitting there inventing an anti-nookie serum I could spray on the sheets to lighten my load. Anyway, shouldn't you get going before the going gets you? You did plenty complaining about the going being tough, making your meeting on time, and now you're going to be late with nothing to keep you here.' Chastised, I would gather my papers and bag and make towards the door, reluctance dragging my heels at the prospect of some of the problems mooted on the agenda. By now I was deeply involved in committees and boards dedicated to improving the tourism product in our area.

'Now, don't rush off just yet.' And I would stop, innocently asking, 'What is it, Connie?'

'Before you go, I just wondered if you sorted out that...' going into a subject that had already taken up vast amounts of our time, to which she knew we had yet to find the solution.

'Are you mad? I never gave it another thought. I can't start working out that just now. Look at the time.'

'Well just remember, when you're spending so much of your time sorting out other people's problems, that this is the place that matters in the long run,' and off she would sail, a knowing smile on that wise face. She knew better than any, even than Himself, who spent so much of his time away, that nights were spent on tourism matters that had little to do with my own establishment and a lot to do with the problems of others; hours spent on the telephone sympathising with callers and diplomatically avoiding being immersed in altercations that had less to do with Tourist Board requirements and more to do with attitudes that had to change before any progress could be made. That time could have been put to good use sorting out some of my own problems. The difficulty was in deciphering whether the attitude belonged to the inspector or the proprietor.

A burning desire to see bed and breakfast recognised as a valuable economic driver in an area so dependent upon the tourism pound drove me on, allied with a hate of the unfairness that prompted some of the calls. The outrageous behaviour of one business against many who did bed and breakfast in a particular community would have taken a Harley Street psychiatrist to sort out. When I refused to indiscriminately take their side and act against the others, some of whom I knew to be totally innocent, I too became the receiver of some pretty vicious attentions.

During one of their many run-ins with 'authority' this couple informed a chief executive that they had friends in the SAS and it would be easy for one of them to come up here and 'take her out'! I couldn't help but laugh when he eventually told me. He had been rather alarmed that I would take the matter seriously and involve him in litigation he could do well without, such were their threats and such was their reputation – and he certainly knew, from their long rant, that they did not mean out to dinner!

I grin every time I think of a B&B wifie being removed from the scene by an SAS hit squad. Laughter was the only answer, though at least three people – which is a large number in a small community with a natural reluctance to seek medical attention for matters of the mind – were so stressed by the attention of this dominating pair that they sought treatment from their local practitioner. I never heard of any others who were threatened by the SAS, even though some were easier targets. I absolutely refused to be bullied and studiously ignored the letters, the staking out of the house, the recorded conversations when 'spies' were sent to my door, and all the other tactics designed to intimidate.

It was a very bad time though. Never in 20 years of working with the high number of people who came into the B&B sector had I come across such crass behaviour. New to the area, they made their mark in ways that few understood. But eventually a change took place that allowed peace to reign supreme. Today the law has changed to give better protection to the harassed victims of such people.

Another of Connie's sayings that entered into daily use was, 'What we will.' If a job had been put off and she found time, she would say, 'We'll do it today... what we will'; or if doubt was cast on whether something was a good idea, she would happily assert, 'We'll give it a go today, what we will.' This was always said with an affirmative nod and a cheerful smile, with the effect of making whatever lay ahead an adventure rather than a trial.

Many a function I attended to find Margaret, Viscountess Thurso, seeking me out. I was of little or no importance to her but she assiduously bore towards me for one purpose only: to enquire after the health of her dear Connie, for whom she had the most tremendous respect. We were both well aware how very fortunate I was to have such a person take control of things when I was furthering the cause of tourism – or as Himself would say, 'When you're off skiving again!'

Thumping into the kitchen and dumping a pile of wet towels beside the washing machine, Connie would seriously ask, 'Could you not try and persuade some of them to stand outside and be hosed down on fine mornings like this?' Not a smile would flicker over her face. 'Think of the work it would save us: no wet towels, no showers to clean, no hairs to chase' could be heard as she disappeared back to the bedrooms. Another time it might be, 'Now, if we put out sleeping bags, the older ones could lie on top of the beds and the younger ones would be fine on the floor. Just think of the work it would save. No sheets to wash and iron, no duvets to change. No beds to make, just a sleeping bag to shake out – only occasionally, mind you. We'll try suggesting it, what we will.'

She could make this amusing aside about cutting down work with the greatest of confidence, as her training and ability ensured our home sparkled. It would have to, as my own standards were known in a country area where word got about faster than I could during my apprentice years. A guest returned from a day out to pass on greetings from a hotelier living at the other side of the county: 'Mrs Mackay is asking for you.' She smiled, adding, 'she was asking if you are still as immaculate as ever!' That was a very long time ago, before anyone came to work with me, and if I was classed immaculate then my close friend Barbara, who spent years with me helping to make our place into the kind of destination I had in mind as I ploughed forward, was meticulous in her ability to turn a home into a shining palace. Suppose you scoured the country from one end to another, you would never find anyone who had Barbara's ability to make things sparkle. She moved through the house in a storm of dusters and polish with her best mate, the vacuum, and would not listen when I said, 'You don't have to check every drawer every day.'

'The day you don't check will be the day something nasty is left.' And she was right. Barbara never worked the weekends and occasionally I would not check, to be confronted by a guest who waved about a pair of knickers, or some such indelicate item, found in a drawer. So when Barbara rushed open the drawers, shutting them, all 30 odd, with a bang, after a quick flick of the duster round each, I knew all was well. A hair would not dare to defy her. Her loyalty, like her work, was beyond reproach and when she retired, it was with a heavy heart that I sought a replacement.

My cousin Diane, the lovely Diane, as gentle as she was kind, who could produce the most scrumptious dinners, joined me for three busy years before taking up a full-time career, leaving me believing I would never get anyone else who would care for the guests and cook for them like she could. Her sympathetic understanding of my many different situations turned work into a pleasure, her wise counsel being as valuable as her care for all who stepped through our door.

And then Connie came, her first job after a long spell of ill health, and neither of us knew how it would work out. Almost on her first day, her worth was proven when she stayed on instead of taking her hours off in the afternoon because she thought a sheep was showing signs of trouble during lambing, and I, as usual, was late in returning from a meeting. She thought nothing of taking full responsibility for dinners so Himself and myself could get a few precious hours off together, her presence like a magic wand that wove laughter and lightness into every day. I pounced on her cooking skills as eagerly as I delighted in her housekeeping ones.

I feel myself thrice blessed. I had three such excellent helpers, as well as Cathy and Rena, who eased the burden of work when it became too much for the regulars as my tourism work took me further and further afield. I hope my appreciation was reflected in a rate of pay far above that of the hotels.

The usual low pay for such important work has given the Scottish hospitality industry a mountain to climb if it wants to compete with the rest of the world in standards of service. This can only be done by employing capable people interested in the tremendous satisfaction arising from genuine service, instead of gap fillers looking to subsidise state handouts, as began to appear when the old stalwarts left and were not replaced through in-house training. Before the advent of the statutory minimum wage, and indeed after it too, the job was so poorly paid and the hours were so unsociable that young people refused to take on what they saw as menial work in what had yet to be recognised as a growing tourism industry.

When I first found the courage to get on my feet to give an

opinion while attending a Tourist Board annual general meeting in the '70s, the first thing I wanted to attack was the low pay in the service industry, emphasising that without addressing the pay scales, we would never get the service that the more discerning visitor now expected. I was lambasted by hoteliers I knew well and respected, who insisted there was no way they could pay staff higher wages with their overheads. It was all right for me; I could employ a couple of people part-time easily enough. I did not have their high costs.

'Nor do I have your opportunities,' I insisted, 'when you can tap into the revenues coming from your well-attended bars, your newly-emerging bar lunches, so popular with low-earning customers. You have the chance to provide set lunches, dinners, high tea and afternoon teas, as well as the morning coffees that the visitor loves to find and is willing to pay for.' But I was incapable of being heard then. I did not have the oratory skills or the weight behind my voice to get any who cared to listen. I felt chastened and wondered if I would ever dare to open my mouth publicly again.

When we went into the car park after that meeting, I watched the two hotel proprietors who were most vociferous in their objections to my desire to see a decent wage climb into their respective Jaguar and BMW while I headed for my old Ford. For me, that spoke volumes, and I determined to hone my argument through whatever means I could to further the cause of tourism.

In that respect, I always had my fledgling business to practice on, and in that field I was well supported, but only after my family accepted that just possibly, just maybe, with a fair stretch of the imagination, Joan did actually work. I was well known within the family as a credible worker but that was a far cry from the respectability of earning a wage with a recognised employer. My gallant helpers were different. They sure knew that Joan worked!

After a particularly hard-going breakfast, in our over-heated kitchen, Connie would stop and say, 'Have you ever asked them if they would just take a sandwich, a bacon one, as they're leaving? You could hand them a couple of hard-boiled eggs... bacon and eggs as they hand you their money. Think of the work it would save...' until I came up with the standard reply, 'We can but ask, we can but ask.'

That last phrase entered into our vocabulary and many a problem was eased by an agreed, 'We can but ask, we can but ask.' I could sometimes hear Connie, who always had a lot of time for the guests, stop in her work to answer some ridiculous question with, 'We can but ask, we can but ask,' and through to the office she would go, face deadpan, to reiterate what to her was a foolish request – usually from an American, most of whom spent their holidays asking a bombardment of questions. They are very serious about thoroughly preparing for their vacations and I am now convinced they have a pre-set selection of questions for each host, regardless of the situation they find on the ground. Such questions are still seriously presented, taken from a huge store and used in order to retain your attention for the maximum period possible. One thing I will say though: they do listen to the answers, not like so many English visitors, who pose the question and answer it themselves before going on to the next one, while you're left opening and closing your mouth like a stranded fish. However, my English guests are the mainstay of my business and without their general good humour I would never have survived for all of 40 years in the trade.

Rushing about, preparing to leave, I hear the transatlantic drawl, 'Do you think we could take a piece of peat, Connie?'

'We can but ask, we can but ask,' comes the patient reply.

'And Connie, do you still use water from the wells? Do you think we could taste it?'

'We can but ask, we can but ask.' The peat was no problem. There was a stack of it outside, though there wouldn't be if everyone wanted a bit, but they were welcome. The water from the well that she had declined to inform them was non-existent, she could deal with, I thought as I grabbed the necessary and shot out the back door, to hear her saying as I sneaked under the open kitchen window, 'The bird has flown. It was here a minute ago and now it's gone...' Knowing Connie, who hated to disappoint, she probably went out to 'the shed' to fill a glass from one of the mineral waters in the stockpile and asked them to sample that. She wouldn't tell a lie. She would just say, 'What do you think of that then?' and await the amazed enjoyment of the purity in our water.

I often came home to be greeted with, 'Well, it's dead, well and truly dead this time. It gave up the ghost. It doesn't want a stay of execution and it doesn't want a resurrection.' It could be anything, but the last before Connie's final season with me was the washing machine that ground to an ignominious halt just as all the rooms required a full change-out.

She found me hurling insults at the silent machine, intent upon getting an admittance that it had saved its mutiny for the most effective moment and that it knew yesterday had been the repair man's day in our area – after all, it had demanded his attentions often enough.

'We'll sort it out, what we will,' she quietly came to the rescue, insisting all washing be taken to her home until the miracle of repair was performed again. There were times it was the dryer, or the dishwasher, or anything else that had struggled on under expensive persuasion to listen to reason and at least try to make it to the end of the season. Some were obliging, some were not, but when Connie certified them dead, there was no denying it; the remains were carted off and the replacement quickly installed, to be greatly admired by me and scolded by her, for not being near so good as its predecessor. She was very loyal.

'How's it going, Connie?' I queried, meeting her in the corridor.

'You don't want to know, though I suppose I've seen jock-straps in funnier places,' and before I could find out more she quickly rounded on me: 'Now listen. Do you think you could stop buying toilet rolls with legs on them? I am sick of putting out spares one day and next day they've walked.' With that she was gone to the next room.

She had a point though. When I first started in B&B I was told, you must put this away and you must hide that, but I left in place the very few valuables we had and was never let down ever, except over a small ornamental dish brought back by my sister Muriel from a holiday in Shetland, which had a fat little Shetland pony depicted on the inside. When two young children shared the room, the dish vanished. I was quite disappointed, but other than the propensity for toilet rolls to go missing, nothing else ever walked. I have to say though, discernment must be taken into consideration, because, should you run out of high-quality loo paper and be forced to stick out an inferior brand, you will find those low-budget rolls are not worthy of souvenir status; they definitely come minus the legs!

A colleague stopped using that particular brand beloved of Labradors because of their tendency to leg it, insisting there were never any puppies she could blame, so it had to be the guests.

10

Entertaining the Mothans

SUCH STATEMENTS AS, 'You better watch the French; they'll help themselves to anything not tied down' have proved rubbish. 'You can't trust the Italians; they'll have someone else sleeping under the bed, and nick food from the table for them' was nonsense, and 'The Germans carry their lunch boxes, getting to the table first and filling them up for the rest of the day's needs, and if you have seats at table overlooking great views, they leave their jackets on the chairs the night before,' was a wicked lie.

You're told you cannot categorise people, but you can observe a national tendency towards a certain behavioural pattern that identifies a visitor as being, for example, American – but America is a big country, as they're fond of telling us. After so many years of close proximity with people and their temperamental peculiarities, none is better qualified than a bed and breakfast operator to lay claim to easily identifying a person's origins. I find there are two distinct types of American attitude, characterised by geography – the Southern States and the Northern States. Give me the guest from the South any day of the week! They have that warm embracing nature that makes their stay a pleasure. Their Northern cousins are different, though most give you as many reasons to be happy to say hello as you are to say goodbye.

Take the French, although initially I would much rather have left them – preferably on the other side of the Channel, shrugging their collective Gallic shoulders in sad reflection of the poor food, poor accommodation, poor manners and everything else they found beneath their standards. This they would usually proceed to do two minutes after meeting you, without having the grace to see what you had to offer before they lambasted in shrugging exaggerated angst, punctuated with heartfelt sighs, every disconsolate experience of their holiday to date. The men's mouths turned down at the corners at the prospect of having to spend a night in your home, their heavily made-up wives cast suspicious glances all around, and this before they came over the threshold!

That they reappeared later all smiles and complimentary gesticulations never quite made up for their earlier rudeness, but this was a very long time ago and attitudes, like facilities, have changed for the better.

It's all very well for Her Majesty and the centenary celebrations of the *Entente Cordiale*, but at least she conceded to previous misunderstandings with our French cousins, though she would not have been referring to problems that arose when the newly-emerging European market sought succour in the beds of our northern counties' proprietors. We met the Germanic tribes with open arms, appreciating their enthusiasm for our remoteness, their cleanliness and their meticulous time keeping, whereas the French, with their shrugs of indifference, their decidedly mucky habits and total disregard for anything smacking of a timepiece, puzzled us.

One neat little French couple wanted to stay for a week, and with no pre-bookings in those days, I explained they would have to spend the first night in a smaller room. Unfortunately I forgot to mention that our resident cat tapped on that particular window seeking sanctuary whenever the mood took her, having once been encouraged into the bed of a single gentleman who desired company in the night. She thought it a fine lark and repeated it at unpredictable intervals, despite my every discouragement. You have to be able to negotiate with cats and I appear to have no bargaining power.

I assured our French guests they would be changed next morning to a large bedroom with fantastic views overlooking the bay. Next day, ready to make the change, I tentatively knocked on their door.

The gentleman waved his hands indignantly. 'Why you want to take our nice room? We happy here Madam!'

Thinking of their comfort, I insisted, 'But you couldn't swing a cat in here!'

'Swing ze cat?' he looked aghast. 'Why you swing cat in our nice room? She a nice... she a good cat.' His indignation on behalf of his newfound feline friend was something to behold. 'You very cruel, Madam. You put cat out in rain. Very bad for cat! Cat cry. Very sad sound. Meiooooooooou! When cat want in, cat come in! We very sorry for poor cat.' Visions of white sheets covered in muddy paw marks and black fur began to take over from my anxiety about their comfort.

Nothing could part them from the room or the cat. Soon afterwards, despite the downpour, Monsieur insisted on going fishing, so he was handed a grape and introduced to the delights of the dung-heap, while his beautiful and glamorous wife waited patiently, sitting like an elf on the steps of the stable, face streaming with rain. The cat? No doubt she was tucked up, warm and cosy, in their bed.

Their bedraggled reappearance – he having amassed a squirming ball of fat worms, she dripping wet, hair plastered to her face – was met with concern, which he cast aside with a laconic shrug, announcing to all, 'She look just like cabbage soup!' It was later discovered that she understood English very well but maintained her dignity by refusing to acknowledge a single spoken word in the face of his irascible comments.

After a day spent in the pouring rain she headed straight for a hot tub, while he went directly to my kitchen, where he insisted on gutting, in my pristine preserve, a massive bag of tiny, smelly tiddlers that no self-respecting person would dream of eating, leave alone fishing out of the burn. I was busy preparing a Taste of Scotland dinner but no amount of Scottish persuasion could match his Gallic indifference and prevent him from performing this nauseating task alongside my intricate preparation for what I intended to be a first class meal.

'I'm preparing your dinner and want to use the sink area and I need it clean,' I foolishly persisted, only prolonging the inevitable. 'You can easily clean the fish outside.' They were tiny, slimy, horrid things.

'Madam, you very cruel lady. You put cat out in rain. You now put me out in rain. I not go. I bigger than cat,' he added quietly, before giving a belligerent, 'I clean fish here. I be quick!' He was not. His tongue never stopped, and having a temperamental Frenchman gutting fish whilst quizzing you about your cooking abilities – or lack of, as his comments implied – is not an ideal situation when you are the sole person responsible for the provision of a quality meal for ten guests. The cat, milling about expectantly at the feet of her friend, did not help matters. Her decision to join proceedings and loudly proclaim her interest in his fish did not go down as well as one might have supposed, considering they slept together the previous night.

'Why don't you give the fish to Felix,' I cajoled, to no avail.

'She a boy cat?' He looked highly indignant. 'You say she a girl cat. Felix! That a boy cat's name. She look like a girl cat. She purr like a girl cat and sleep all night like a girl cat. Madam, did you let a boy cat sleep in our bed?' He was frowning at the cat, his head cocked to a side.

For goodness sakes! *He* let the cat sleep in his bed. What did it matter whether she was a boy or a girl cat? Felix had been named when I had believed she was a tom; she proved otherwise, but try telling that to this man who was taking over my kitchen, now more concerned about the gender of a cat than my spoiling dinner.

'She,' I emphasised with renewed vigour, determined to get rid of him, 'a girl cat. OK?'

'You very cruel lady, giving girl cat a boy's name,' he managed before proudly demanding his catch be cooked for breakfast – everyone's. 'All us people's breakfasts... and none for zis gridee cat,' who was patiently waiting her share of such gastronomic delights.

Next morning I had little option but to crisp fry a platter, which was placed on the middle of the breakfast table for any to partake of after being served their normal order. This must have been a considerable time ago, yet I still remember our conversations, and being astounded to be told by most of the guests round the table that the fish were the sweetest and nicest they had tasted. The 'gridee' cat was not offered a morsel and promptly removed her affection elsewhere for the duration of her erstwhile friend's stay.

They were actually amongst the best of the few French visitors we saw in those early days, and it took time to learn the ways of the French and provide for their individual needs, they being a nation that did not hold with 'When in Rome, do as the Romans do'. For years now, our establishment has been highlighted in *Le Guide du Routard*, one of the many foreign publications in which we are delighted to have accolades, never knowing how we get there nor paying a penny towards our inclusion. We enjoy the business and welcome the mainly French guests who swear by this guide. Sadly, the French have a tendency towards leaving things too late, so that with only three rooms on offer now we turn away many enquiries, being already booked out. But each time I hear that attractive accent, I am reminded of my irascible Frenchman and zat gridee cat!

When German visitors first began to knock on the door, their ways were hard to accept. They were obtrusively demanding in ascertaining all was to their satisfaction. Once satisfaction was established, they were really good to have in your home, but the initial approach made their attitude difficult to deal with, especially with me being young and inexperienced, wanting only to please my paying guest and much in awe of their commandeering attitude and insistence on securing the best at the cheapest rate possible. I adamantly refused to barter over price, convinced guests were getting a fantastic deal, and I would just as soon turn away those who wanted to bargain on the doorstep. Today, we are encouraged to do last-minute deals, but way back then, dropping rates to catch the passing trade appeared mercenary and disloyal to neighbouring B&Bs. Oh, did I have a lot to learn – and usually I learned the hard way when I discovered how others viewed the field. I was genuinely surprised to be told by a Tourist Information Centre member of staff that just about every other B&B in the area checked with her what I was charging, before setting their own rate somewhat below mine. She thought I should consider it a compliment, their belief I had gauged it about right! What I did think was that the Tourist Board should have given a steer to members unsure of what to charge. To this day, there never has been such guidance.

Like most men of my parent's generation, my father had fought in World War II, as an officer in the Royal Navy. My mother, the youngest of a family of six, had seen her older brother swallowed up in the fields of the Great War. She lived in a small coastal community of about seven households, each of which had lost one or more male members of the family to the enormity of that war. World War II gave her plenty to worry about, with her husband at sea and his parents as well as a growing family to care for and feed. As far as the German nation was concerned, she was much less forgiving than my father, who had a certain respect for the officers of the navy of his enemy. He knew the German navy had little to do with the worst atrocities of the war and his natural instinct was to admire courage, dedication and skill, characteristics which were to play a great part in the life he chose after his war years. He believed his German counterparts had these attributes and during his rare times at home, the books beside his bed told as much of the leaders of his enemy as they did of his great hero, Sir Winston Churchill. My mother gave those books to me after his unexpected and sudden death in 1974, and I treasure them.

Our parents were frequent callers at the homes of both Sandra and I, being the first of their five children to marry. Often when they called on me, I had 'nighters' in the house, something that did not entirely meet with my mother's approval. She could let you know exactly what she thought of a situation without opening her mouth. She was a handsome woman in the true sense of the word and had a way with her mouth, eyebrows, eyes and tilt of the head that required no voiceover. Even now I shudder at the memory of meeting her in the corridor, heading for our sitting room, where she enquired most imperiously, 'Joan, have you got Krauts in the house?'

Aaaaahhhhhh! Eyes like saucers, I all but manhandled her into our private quarters. 'They'll hear you!' The German couple were in their bedroom and would need to be deaf not to have heard. 'What of it?' was her nonchalant rejoinder, and as far as she was concerned, they were not worth the consternation. Not that their English was good, for in those days we got the older generation and few spoke fluent English. They were not the easiest of people to work with; nevertheless I was determined to offer every courtesy. My mother was not, but over the years, when younger specimens found their way north, with their lack of guilt or blame, and my father engaged in avuncular conversations, she gave in to a grudging acceptance. Such was Dad's popularity among the few guests who met him, one Danish couple – the first to introduce us to accepting relationships that had yet to be blessed by the church in a double-bedded room – when they did marry called their son Magnus in his honour.

This was in the days when standards of facilities, if not morals, were happily relaxed and we partied with our guests. The young Continentals, as we fondly referred to any who crossed the channel, were tremendously pleased to join in such fun. We had one German group of four friends, all teachers, who stayed all of a month, during which many things happened. But my abiding memory is of them all traipsing back from the harbour with sea urchins. We used to all sit on the wall which separated the vast vegetable garden from the back-door patio, drinking the home-made wine Sally and I had put down in the spring, when we had dragged ourselves away from the horses to fill baskets of whin flowers, determined to master the art of wine-making.

My memory is of astonishment, when I came back from the shop to find them all sitting, legs astride the wall, scraping the spines off the shellfish into the veg garden, without a thought of the consequences. It might have been fine food for the vegetables, but the stench was all-pervading long after they left the premises! It was a scorching hot summer, as were so many in the '70s and '80s, though few have been of late.

We still see people from all over the world and still believe we can suss out countries of origin by virtue of their nature. Especially prior to email, many people would just arrive on your doorstep on the pure chance of you having a room.

'What are they?'

Refusing to give in to temptation and say, 'People, guests, what did you think they were?', I give the expected country-of-origin reply: 'Canadians, I think. They have to be, they are so nice.' Of course, it turns out they are Americans.

Again, 'What are they?' has me saying, 'Bloody Australians. No way are they New Zealanders with an attitude like that.'

An hour after, a changed attitude – as usually happens after people have had time to chill out and take in the premises – invites the question, 'Which area of Australia do you hail from?', which elicits the contemptuous reply, 'Do you mind! New Zealand. We're from New Zealand.' So it's little wonder I get nervous when asked to say from which country my latest last-minute guests have originated.

Quite recently Himself, in a moment of magnanimity, took pity on my speeding form as I tried to vacuum and answer constant phone calls at the same time. Grabbing the cleaner he offered, 'I'll do that for you.'

'Listen,' I warned, 'The mothans, in Room 2 – it will take a bit of effort to shift them,' as I rushed for the office to catch another call before the answerphone clicked on.

'Well, I haven't got all day,' I heard as I disappeared for the next half hour.

Meeting him in the corridor with vacuum still in hand and an exasperated look on face, I asked what was wrong.

'It's that Mothans, they're never like to shift!'

'Tell me about it,' I sympathised. 'I get that every other day of the week and short of physically removing them one by one, there isn't another answer if the Hoover doesn't do the trick.'

'Ah, I see.' His look changed to one of growing under-standing. 'You get going with the hoovering in the empty bed-rooms so the likes of the Mothans will take the hint and get going too.'

'Pardon?' It was me now who was failing to grasp the line of thinking.

'Letting the Mothans know you have to get in there at some time to do their room.' Annoyance was back in supremacy.

I looked at him, blinking, for a good 10 seconds as he con-tinued to grapple with the wrong end of the stick.

'Where is Mothan, anyway? I've never heard of it. You said yesterday they were Spaniards and I checked the book for their name and it certainly sounded Spanish to me. Is it somewhere in Spain?'

One thing I know, you do not offend the help when you are not paying them, especially when they have taken on extra work, so I smothered my laughter to say very seriously, 'Have you never ever heard of mothans?'

'No, and I don't believe such a place exists.' His geography was far superior to mine, we both knew. 'People could come from Mexico and you would have me believe they were from Mars.'

'You know those little flecks of fluff that stick to the carpets, from woolly socks and flannelette pyjamas?' I waited confirmation that he knew what I was talking about.

With my speed and carelessness and his deafness, mutual incomprehension is typical and, to our family's continuing delight, highly entertaining.

'Oh, god!' I cried. This time I did not dissolve into laughter. 'They *are* the Corrals and they *do* come from Spain, and mothans are the bits of fluff I wanted to make sure you vacuumed off the carpet. Right?'

'Mothans! I never heard the likes. Mothans! Is it Gaelic?'

'Well, I didn't make it up just to confuse you, so it probably is. I grew up hearing about mothans and the first chance I get with Sandra I'll be checking that one out.'

It was he who was in fits of laughter now, as I headed off to scrutinise the carpet... for mothans!

11

New Tricks for the Old Dog

'YOU CAN'T TEACH an old dog new tricks.'

'Yes, you can,' I insisted, 'providing the dog knows his work pays for his supper. I learn new tricks every day. I even had to learn to use both hands to do different jobs at the same time to get everything done quickly enough.'

'Exactly my point.'

'Meaning?'

'Everything you do. You're just making work for yourself.' This time he was brandishing a fistful of silver cutlery, lifted off the table when I showed how I set it for breakfast. Dinner was already a thing of the past some time before he filtered into taking over so many of the tasks when Connie made the regrettable decision she would no longer be able to work with me.

'There's people having fish as well as grills!' My voice rose a few decibels, just in case it was his tendency towards deafness causing the problem and not a stubborn refusal to conform to what he called my unnecessary extravagances in both time and effort. Between fortnights away and the pile-up of work awaiting his return to the croft, he had been kept in fair ignorance of the practical side of my work.

My years with Connie had been by far the best in the business, for many different reasons, and the laughter we shared on a daily basis can evoke powerful nostalgia when I slip down memory lane. Though I was happy to find a replacement for Connie, Himself suggested I did not, and anyway, Connie, with her skills, her love of people and animals, and her easy working manner was irreplaceable, of that there was no doubt. But then, I had thought the same of Barbara, who was replaced by Diane, whose high standards convinced me she too was indispensable.

My bold husband insisted he would fill the gap! After all, he had been taking on more and more of the role while I kept the post open in the hope that Connie's recurring ill health would, in time, allow her to come back. Sadly, this did not happen. And my insistence on keeping the business going while fighting cancer; didn't he show his willingness to lend a hand then? 'Yes, but we had Connie then,' I argued. Stubbornly he insisted, 'I would work fine with Diane or Barbara or Connie, but no way can an old dog like me learn to work with some-one new. Old dogs just don't learn new tricks!'

'Well, old dogs better curb their appetite for fine malts then,' was my only rejoinder.

The breakfast table had looked splendid in its snowy white linen and fine china, finished off in an array of sparkling silver cutlery to suit the variety of dishes that awaited the guests' attention. The old dog's objection to laying down fish forks and knives as well as meat cutlery at every place had been voiced before, but I took no heed. It looked good, and saved the hassle of changing cutlery according to whether it was a meat or a fish dish placed in front of the guests when they chose their seating in the morning.

He argued long and hard and won the day. I gave in and said I would follow hotel procedure and lift the unwanted cutlery when the requested dish was set before the diner. But I kept forgetting and he had a better idea. The table would be set with meat knives and forks only and he would diligently leave the requisite fish cutlery for me to exchange for that already set. 'What's wrong with that?' he indignantly asked, a phrase I have become more and more familiar with. I muttered many bad words below his hearing level, which does fluctuate according to perceived interest.

Why did I find this such a difficult task? Because I had to remember to pick up the fish cutlery, neatly waiting at the end of the table, and that would only go well if, before that, I remembered to keep one hand free to complete the operation. That was fine, provided first I arranged the fish dish in true waitress fashion, resting on the left arm while another plate was balanced on the curve of the left wrist, with the right hand holding a meat- or egg-orientated course, ready to be set down in front of the guest. Then, and only then, would my right hand be free to pick up the fish cutlery, which I could deftly transfer to the waiting fingers of my left hand, then with free right hand remove the meat cutlery that was no longer required, repeating this action with the next person ordering fish. Did you follow that? No? It's madness! Go on, try it and see for yourself, with a table of discerning dinner guests if you are not in a position to experiment with paying guests at breakfast. That should focus the mind and prove my point.

The skill is in remembering the sequence and the art is in not grabbing the meat cutlery out of the hand of the guest who dares to lay a finger upon it before you can do your conjuring trick; suchlike capers are not on the breakfast menu and are best performed by Basil Fawlty. If they prove perverse and exercise their right to put meat cutlery to fish dish, you just saunter out of the dining room, subtly hiding the offending fish cutlery, as if you never intended they use the correct cutlery – a trick learned from the cats. They are experts at pretending an unintended outcome was their original intention.

You also ignore any comments you may hear as to why

so-and-so got presented with fish cutlery for their fish course, when they, eating fish as well, were allowed to continue with meat cutlery. You never admit to having got your sequence so badly wrong that the guest got stuck in before you could change the cutlery.

Does any of that worry the man behind the removal of the cutlery? Not one bit. The easy answer would be to forget that fish cutlery exists, but having bought it, at great expense, albeit years ago and to serve dinners, it seems a pity for it to languish in a drawer, tarnishing. During one inspector's visit, it was one thing – possibly the only thing – that impressed her. And if it were banished from the table, it would be yet another lost cause in my insistence that certain standards be kept. It would also be a great blessing, but I have yet to find a way to bring that blessing about without losing face.

Taking real note of what was going on for the first time, he objected to many things he thought to be outwith the bounds of need, yet happily proffered tea and home-made cakes to every guest upon arrival, regardless of time, setting out a silver tray with silver coffee, tea and hot water pots, cakes and shortbread on small china plates with napkins neatly folded, appropriate sugars for coffee and tea in place, which meant bowls and silver sugar spoons, never once succumbing to the temptation to use those little packets of brown and white sugar. Never a hint of exasperation, never a look of 'I could be doing something important on the croft just now' crossed his welcoming face. I had been lax, so he told me. I had only offered this welcoming gesture until some vague notion of evening indicated it was no longer necessary, and sometimes, using my judgement, which he said was prone to many mitigating factors, I did not mention tea at all.

'They didn't look as if they wanted tea,' was not acceptable, I was indignantly told. It was not in my advertising, and I viewed it as a pleasant surprise, but such unreliable, erratic behaviour horrified my new help. Even after years of toeing the line, he still asks, 'Did you offer tea?' Yes, I always do now, even at midnight. 'And did you put out the napkins?' Ah, well, maybe I forgot. He knows me well. I would have been too busy talking.

I see this service now as an opportunity to exceed expectations, doing it gladly, with a little help from the old dog, who never fails to have the kettle on the minute the doorbell rings.

But today he eyed me suspiciously as he unlocked Room 2. 'You've not been in this room yet?'

'Not yet,' I agreed, nonplussed. 'I wanted to complete the other rooms first.' Being somewhat older than I, and governed by routine, his work pattern is doggedly adhered to, while I multi-task my way from kitchen to office, cooker to bedroom, the garden, the dining room, the lounge, and the sitting room, between mad dashes to the greenhouse or the 'shed', as Connie called our storehouse-cum-garage, filled with the backup of necessities ready to meet all expectations and outperform all competition, and store guests' bikes, these things being far more important than housing any car we ever owned. There are times when I must look like a demented lemming heading for the cliffs, but, on this occasion as on most others, I was not about to admit any lapse in judgement or memory.

This lack of method in my madness suits my nature and at the end of the day a great deal is achieved, but it does entail a few shocks here and there, and castigations when it is discovered that certain duties have not been carried out. It appeared I had not only acquired a help-mate but a boss who cheerfully went *his* way about *my* business, after glibly announcing, 'OK, you know best yourself,' then doing what he liked.

'Then why...?' but, with time at a premium, the finer points of domesticity lay unchallenged, one-upmanship and hierarchical order in the workplace never particularly worrying either of us, our marriage always being a shared 'you do what you can and I'll do what I can' sort of union.

12

Tooth and Nail

MOST OF US have read *It Shouldn't Happen to a Vet* and I'm sure there are copy-cat versions relating to doctors, policemen, teachers and what have you. Well, you can rest assured, It Shouldn't Happen to a B&B Wifie, either. The strange nature of the job is, at times, asking for the inevitable to happen. With a bit of restraint, most incidents should never have happened to me, but restraint, like due diligence, is alien to my personality.

Tales of woe bubble to the surface but to put them in sequence may prove difficult and in any case chronology adds nothing to the 'happenings' (as our flower-power friends of the '60s would call them). The value of dragging such things back to the forefront of the mind could be in the advice, whether to prospective guests or proprietors of establishments, that the road to a red face can usually be avoided – though at times, because you are dealing with the vagaries of human nature and yourself at your most capricious, events do take on a life of their own.

You may be tempted to look back on these events and laugh, but no matter how relieved you are the event is behind, you mustn't be tempted to dine out on your *faux pas*; in fact, don't tell a living soul. Should the public get one whiff of the wrong end of the stick, you will find yourself accused of all sorts of inadequacies that bear only a passing resemblance to the reality of your original slip. Don't say a word! Not unless retirement is beckoning. That's why I'm telling you now.

With such incidents well behind me, and the prospect of being exposed for a fraud and a charlatan no longer looming large in my nightmares, I can reflect with wonder at how they came about. Sometimes it seems as if the world is out to get me, or perhaps one of the toes I once trod upon had a hotline to the Karma King, for someone is surely taking pleasure out of my mortification.

Many years ago, before car seatbelts became mandatory, while dashing to a meeting, a rabbit shot out and I braked hard. Even though I grew up as a bit of a tomboy, the prospect of killing wild rabbits could never be contemplated. When they appeared at table in a very palatable stew I had to force myself not to think of them wearing little blue jackets, or of my mother as a pie-making Mrs McGregor. In adult life, braking for rabbits became instinctive, resulting that day in a severely cracked tooth, which I had to have capped. But ever afterwards, every now and again, the cap would come out.

On one such occasion, with breakfast to serve before I could visit the dentist that afternoon, pride insisted that I greet my guests with my usual smile and chatter. To meet and greet in silence was not an option as they knew from the night before that talking came very naturally to me. A temporary replacement of the tooth sometimes works and sometimes doesn't, and on this occasion it did. Felt secure. I was happy.

It was only when I returned to the kitchen after serving the last dish that I felt the ominous gap in my mouth. Shock, horror and a certain amount of awe got my full attention.

I sat down heavily to assess the situation. How could it have come out without me knowing? I always knew when the tooth moved position and had never lost it before. Visions of scenes from the dining room did their best to overwhelm me. Which guest would it be? It was bound to have fallen into the food, the most obvious place – when I was concentrating hard on those bloody fish knives, I bet. Who had fish?

Realisation was heart-stopping. It was that woman with the uppity voice whose eyes automatically skimmed every available surface for the merest mote of dust that could be held against you. Even her feet looked fastidious. It would have to be her; sod's law was always exercising its rights over me.

'What's wrong with you?' the man Himself asked, taking in my forlorn form.

'Nothing, nothing at all. Just a quick break.' No way was I telling him.

'Are you sure you're all right? Last time you looked like that was then you lost your nail.'

'What?' My head shot up. I did not want to be reminded of that episode. It had been bad enough, but this was worse. I dwelled on the nail fiasco while I made a surreptitious search of the kitchen, praying I would spot the tooth first – though I'd sooner even he saw it than the guest find it in the fish dish.

My horse had stood on my toe, no doubt to teach me the full effect standing on people's toes can have. Horses always stand on the big toe and look very sorry when you react with a wide-mouthed scream and hysterical jumping up and down. The ensuing spectacle, accompanied by moans and groans, is probably high in their entertainment category and the sorry face is far from genuine. In time, repeated attacks on the toe ensure the nail begins to slowly release its grip as a new one starts to form. It was summertime and, by a mere thread, I hung on to my nail, a good, strong, nicely-cut nail, painted pillar-box red to camouflage the dark blue of the bruising so that the foot still looked good when sandals were worn. Very fussy about my feet, I was, knowing the hard graft they endured each season and how long I intended them to last. Any part going kaput was to be fought against, right to the wire. I had promised Himself that I would reinstate his now denuded bank balance, and I must stay healthy and fit if that goal were ever to be reached.

I was determined my nail would make it to the end of summer and warned my horse that one more casual attempt at eliciting what he obviously saw as a comic turn would land him at the knacker's yard. He had already been on his way to elimination when bought by the chap who called him Bronco and quickly sold him on to me, so the threat held good. He was young and good looking – the horse, not the man – and the trip to near eternity was solicited by his unpredictable behaviour, which marked him as a killer. I found out his dicey equine history after I had fallen in love with him – and he with me, he always assured, though he had a funny way of showing it, as is the way of most males.

'It's gone!' I gasped, glancing down at my feet when I stopped to share an afternoon break with my mentor, Himself.

'What's gone?' he naturally asked, and became alarmed at seeing my eyes widen and mouth drop open as I remembered where I had last seen the nail, seductively peeking through my sandals. The rooms were all serviced now, and occupied by guests who would not welcome intrusion from a wild-eyed woman searching for a missing body part.

It was a good-sized nail, and such a bright obvious red. There was no way it could be optically missed, though it was missed by me as I gazed down in disgust at the half-grown effort left in its wake whilst my imagination ran riot. Could it possibly have flicked up onto a bed as I shook out the duvet? Would it be waiting by a pillow, the white linen a perfect foil to the red? But what if they didn't see it and discovered it by placing a delicate *derrière* upon its sharp corners? Oh, god. What if it came to light by invading even more delicate parts of the anatomy during nocturnal activities?

What then?

The prospects were endless and not one better than the other. It just couldn't have got into the shower, the loo or the wash-hand basin, could it? Maybe the basket of toiletries I had put on the floor whilst cleaning the shelves? Or worse, the tea tray? Oh, yuck!

With a look of complete misery on my face I trailed through the house, eyes downcast, searching, and listening too as I passed each closed door, waiting for the howl of derision – I kept my ears cocked in expectation of it all night.

Next morning, in a pair of sensible shoes despite the heat, I cooked with none of the usual gaiety, nor the satisfaction of a job well done. But the guests were all in the finest of feckle that morning, and it was only when emptying the vacuum that the offensive thing finally reappeared.

Now it all flooded back and paled by comparison to this new catastrophe.

I had got off with the nail. The jammy-side-up law demanded I could not get off with the tooth as well and my heart sank as I prepared to go into the dining room to pick up the plates. The guests were all busy talking and did not seem to notice my close-mouthed scrutiny of each plate lifted. Nor did anyone notice the addition of spectacles to my face, all the better to see with, so I at least would know which guest to avoid for the last short while of their stay. They were all leaving, which was, in itself, a relief, but this meant a vast amount of work to get through before haring off to the dentist. Eric Sutherland never let me down, always managing to give me an appointment when telephoned in despair, 'My tooth's come out and I have a meeting in the afternoon,' or words to that effect – because it purposefully always came out just before an occasion I was to be speaking at. It liked to remind me that it could, if so inclined, fly out during an impassioned plea made round the board table. A tooth that kept me on my toes.

Now I had no tooth to be reinstated. It was not on the breakfast plates, which was a tremendous relief. Would someone hand me a neatly folded paper handkerchief, with a look of dignified disgust on their hurt face, and not even tell me where it had revealed itself? Oh, the horrors of the probabilities made me weak with anxiety, but again the guests bid their happy goodbyes to a strangely quiet host, after which I felt obliged to admit the loss to the man Himself.

Instead of the expected lecture he too began a thorough search of the dining room, from where he suddenly emerged, triumphant, handing me the offending tooth. I leapt for joy, relieved when he said he had found it on the carpet, beside one of the chairs. My reputation saved once again! Mind you, it had come *that* close to entering the food chain in a manner not intended for teeth, but I was greatly cheered to be reunited with my precious piece of porcelain and meekly accepted the rebuke, 'Don't let that ever happen again. That was worse than the nail.'

He had not had even a fraction of the worry of the tooth, only knowing of its loss after the guests had left. Had he thought for one minute I believed it had fallen onto a plate of food, he would have been truly mortified, and abandoned the premises until he felt it safe to come back. I had a dog like that once, who shot off to my in-laws after every outrageous misdemeanour, then sneaked back believing all would be forgiven; and a son who would, when small, after testing the waters to new depths, shout from the top of the hills, 'Is it safe to come home yet?'

I never quite managed to see the funny side of the tooth and nail incidents but I still smile when I think of the stushie I got into one evening. Connie was working along with me, serving dinner to eight guests as we waited for a couple to arrive, Italians, who had booked our last double room.

Stereotyping nationalities can be an occupational hazard. The exception to your own preconceptions always throws you.

But the Italians have to be classed as the best of guests, though very hard work. They seldom travel in couples, preferring the familiarity of the pack, and nearly always arrive late, wanting dinner at unearthly times. Back then I often cooked an evening's third set of dinners for Italians who had charmed me into running after them long past midnight. Even so, they remain to this day my favourite guests.

The Pietros, my expected couple, had not booked dinner. By the time the doorbell rang, our Spanish couple were back in their bedroom and our party of four ensconced in the lounge, with the other couple off for a walk, while Connie stuck in to clearing up after dinner. Himself was safe on the oil rig and well out of it and our son was still serving with the Royal Marines, so I just had myself, the guests and the animals to cater for, with the stalwart help of Connie.

The corridor leading to the bedrooms is closed off from the main hallway opening into the kitchen, dining room and guest lounge, with a very substantial glass fire door that deadens all sound in either direction – which proved just as well.

I answered the front door to find not two, but three Italians standing on the step. I prepared to explain that all our rooms were booked when the woman smiled charmingly and said, 'But we are the Pietros. We booked.'

My heart sank. What kind of mistake had been made here? I always think it is I who makes the error, though it seldom is when taking bookings, my errors concentrating on other areas of life.

My expression must have spoken for me because she immediately assured, 'Do not worry. This, my son. We not expect him to come. He can share our room.' The boy must have been at least twelve, possibly older, and without doubt would require a bed of his own.

'But there's only one double bed in the room you booked,' I explained.

'You put more bed in? In Scotland this not a problem. We see the room?' she smiled while Mr Pietro and son looked on, slightly bemused but smiling also.

En masse we moved towards the room, through the fire door and to the left. I opened the door to the double while I tried to explain that I did not have an extra bed. 'But in Scotland, you find extra beds. Just a leetle one,' she indicated with finger and thumb just how tiny the bed could be, continuing to smile and raise her brows and shoulders in the most persuasive manner.

'The room, it is lovely. We stay here. We all sleep in the one bed, if no other bed,' she decided, having believed me when I said we had no put-you-up bed. It was not exactly true, and with the prospect of them all trying to sleep in a double, I gave thought to the stored spare bed. That was my first mistake.

Connie poked her face round the fire door. 'Are they wanting dinner?'

'No!' I glanced at my watch. It was nine thirty and the days of doing multiple settings of dinners were over.

'Yes,' they said in unison, and Mrs Pietro went on, 'This a nice house. We like dinner too. It is possible?' My mind was in overdrive now, determined to solve the problem. Moving them into the lounge to look at the menu would help.

'Look,' I said. 'Connie will sort out dinner with you and I will find another bed to put up in the room for your son.' I believed it to be a simple task and thought all would be well.

The bed was stored at the back of a cupboard under the stairs. Only one problem. Access to this cupboard was through the room that was now occupied by the Spanish couple. Still, it was only a little after nine thirty and though they were in their room, they would probably soon be joining their dinner companions, whose company they enjoyed. They appeared to have a fair understanding.of English, though their responses were quite pidgin-like.

Connie swept off, with the Pietros whispering to each other, 'See, in Scotland, they find beds. I tell you. It always is true.'

I lightly knocked on the door of the Cantellas' room. Dead silence. Knocking a little louder, my ear close to the door, the faint sounds of rustling could be heard. I was committed now. I had to get that bed. I couldn't even scrub up my own room for the young lad. We had long since bought a caravan to sleep in ourselves and let all five bedrooms in the house.

I gave a sharp rap and stood back. Silence. Then I distinctly heard the rattle of the key firmly asserting its place in the lock. Very reassuring for them, but not for me as I waited, breath held, and not a sound coming from beyond the door.

'Mr Cantellas?' I lightly enquired, knowing that all negotiations with Spaniards must be made through the male, despite him usually being the one with the poorest English. The door slowly opened, a mean two inches, and round its edge came a nose, followed by one coal-black eye. 'What you want?' he hissed.

'I need the bed...' was as far as I got.

'You not get my bed.' The door began to close. I quickly pressed my hand upon it so I could explain. 'I only want the bed...'

'You not *get* my bed.' His voice was clipped with agitation, the one peeping eye now narrowed as he stared into my pleading face. 'Please, Mr Cantellas...' I got out before both eyes and a black tuft of receding hair, Mr Cantellas not being in the first flush of youth, appeared round the door. I could see his little black moustache begin to twitch.

'Look,' I rushed on, my own eyes taking on a wilder appearance, 'Can I please come in? I can explain about the bed.'

He pressed the door harder and hissed louder. By now Connie had appeared and was standing behind me, wide-eyed too. 'You not get my bed! We need bed.' His voice had risen several decibels.

I glanced at Connie in desperation and saw the suspicions

of a smirk. I was losing my communication skills, if not the plot, as I went into pleading mode and started, 'It's for this Italian family, they need an extra bed...'

Outraged, he opened the door a little further, no longer hissing, and shouted, 'My wife, she *need* the bed. She sleep,' and he indicated towards a corner of the bed I could see. By this time Connie had moved position so she also could take a peek in the direction of the pointing hand.

Jet-black curls only could be seen, and then very slowly two wide-open, staring, coal-black eyes appeared above bed-clothes held by two tightly-gripping fists.

That was all Connie needed. She stepped back out of sight, doubled over, and I distinctly heard her saying, 'Manuel! Manuel!' before convulsing into smothered laughter.

I gave Connie a hefty backwards kick. I learned this from the horses. Their tactics came in very handy in times of stress. If she didn't control herself I would turn round and bite her. Instead I made another gallant attempt at retrieving the situation. 'I don't want *your* bed. I want my own bed and it's...'

'Tonight, it not your bed. It *my* bed. I pay for bed.' He opened the door a little further and pointed to the bed. The bedclothes remained firmly held above his wife's nose.

'I know that, I know that,' I said in desperation, 'but the Italians...'

'Italians!' He just about spat. 'Italians not get my bed!'

Putting my shoulder to the door, I glimpsed Connie, who had now reached her knees in a desperate bid to suppress what was becoming hysterical laughter as she gasped, 'Oh, god! Manuel at his best, and he's the spit image!' Her concern was most encouraging, so I hissed back at her, 'Go and see to the Italians in case they come through.' That would be all I needed. The way things were going it was a miracle no one else could hear the increasing volume of the protestations, never mind Connie's laughter.

Giving her a dirty look I said, 'Find out if anyone speaks Spanish, for god's sake!'

'I speak Spanish,' Manuel informed me indignantly from the other side of the door. 'I go now. I sleep,' he emphasised as he made a firm attempt to close the door – but I had my foot well placed by now.

'I have to get in,' I demanded, throwing all caution to the winds and giving the door an almighty shove. The bedcovers were instantly whipped over the head of Mrs Manuel. Immediately behind the bedroom door was the coveted cupboard where the disputed bed lay. I wrenched it open while Manuel danced behind me to the alarming tune of spitting indignation. But I did not care. I was triumphant! 'There,' I hotly contended, feeling a trickle of sweat run down my spine. 'That is the bed I want.'

He stood dead still, eyes widening and hand gripping the top of his pyjama jacket. Realisation swept over his face.

'Ah, Señora. Si! Si! Ze bed, ze bed. You want ze bed. Si! Si!' A big grin of relief quickly spread across his features as he kept nodding and prancing about, helping me wheel ze bed out ze door, giving relieved glances in the direction of his wife's form, still secure under the duvet, and continuing to nod his head and repeat, 'Si! Si! Si, Madam, si,' in the reassuring tones one would use with a deranged, though hopefully not dangerous, person.

'She want ze bed.' His magnanimity filled the room but she was taking no chances and remained firmly covered. Manuel just about clipped my heels as he slammed the door behind me, turning the key in the lock with rattling finality.

Connie had vanished, but it kept us laughing for months whenever any situation involving a bed became fraught. One or the other would only have to say, 'You no get my bed!'

Our animals, too, had a propensity towards giving us red faces, and one of the reddest – there were many – came courtesy of the horses. When Troubie was given to our four-year-old son, as a nine-month-old prize-winning foal, the colt spent a lot of time in the park beneath the front windows, where he learned to play football with the village children and he and his young master took immense pleasure in rolling down a gentle slope while my heart stayed in my mouth, watching spindly legs and solid hooves appear and disappear, dangerously close to the spindly legs and not-so-solid head of our rumbustuous son.

Troubie, a beautiful chestnut part-Arab, took to standing in that field while guests ate in the dining room, with its panoramic views beyond the large picture windows. Oblivious to the views, the pony would delight in flooding the ground with a copious frothy flow, causing amused glances. Then, as he grew older, he preferred to continue with an examination of his own tackle.

Entertaining a business colleague one day, lunching by the window, Troubie soon ambled along and got down to contemplating his bits and pieces. This time he literally got down, lying flat out on the ground, facing the window, giving my guest, a man of superior attitude, much the best perspective. I had to resist the temptation to whisk the curtains across the window in case the poor man believed my motive to be anything other than trying to win more recognition for the B&B sector from the newly-emerging Local Enterprise Company taking over from the Highlands and Islands Development Board. My agenda was, as it still is, putting B&B at the top, though some suspect otherwise.

This was a working croft and the natural behaviour of animals should be expected, but his desire for an audience led to what can only be described as misbehaviour after Troubie welcomed a new stable-mate into his life.

This was four-year-old Bronco, the possessor of the devious mind. Both animals took to gazing up with interest at any form of activity within the confines of the house. This delighted the guests, as both were extremely handsome beasts and no animal can show off quite like a horse.

One always tried to ignore Troubie, now all of 14.2 hh and no longer entire – not quite the same amount of bits and pieces to contemplate. His interest in his own anatomy was not easily dismissed, but the guests did not seem bothered as they discoursed round the table. That was until Bronco made his appearance. You just knew things would go downhill from there.

Knowing the drill, I kept my eyes on the food and the guests, making interesting repartees in the hope it would keep their eyes fixed on the table and their dining companions and not on the pair outside the window. But you could see glances towards the field, some of awe, others quietly knowing and still others with red faces, though not as red as mine. The stable-mates took great delight in indulging in a 'mine is bigger than yours' contest which seemed to go on forever, as did their efforts to see who could put on the best performance. Bronco was more than a full hand higher, which drove Troubie on to supreme efforts. As they vied with each other, they kept glancing up towards the house, as if they would much prefer human arbitration to ascertain the winner. The exuberance and pride with which they accomplished this singularly masculine form of showing off had to be seen to be believed, though, for my money, too many saw it.

I don't remember any comment made by a guest, and certainly not by me, nor did I know how they resolved their chauvinistic disagreement, but eventually they put everything away and maintained their normal dignity, which enthralled the guests and led to a passion for polo mints as my explicit instruction not to give titbits to the horses was furtively disobeyed by all.

Those were only a couple of the many situations brought on by the guile of the horses. The cats and the house rabbits, the odd mouse, and the lambs too, could all drop you in it without a murmur of conscience, not to mention a grandchild who put all the rest in the shade when it came to giving granny a red face.

However, I think you have heard enough for now to confirm your suspicions as to how bed and breakfast is really run. I can see the sage nods and hear declarations of 'I knew it!' as the beans continue to cascade from the can.

13

Gilding the Lily

'THERE'S BLUEDIE DAAYSIES on ti plaate!' the strongly-accented voice followed me out of the dining room. I stopped at the open door, within earshot though unseen. They were the only two guests having a 7am breakfast, succumbing to the lure of a day trip to the Orkney Islands.

If he didn't like t'bluedie daaysies then he would have to blame t'bleudie Tourist Board. Long since was the day they advocated we all adorn our breakfast dishes with weeds – as my three-year-old nephew had put it at his sister's wedding when faced with a nicely-garnished dish.

I was among the many who greeted with dismay this request from our inspectors to add a little more class to a dish by indulging in some culinary art, implacable in my belief there was no herb would go with kippers. And how on earth could you further adorn a plate of so-called traditional breakfast? However, I now lay sprigs of thyme beside the kippers and some guests actually sprinkle the herb on the fish, saying it enhances the flavour. With fish and egg concoctions being very easy to decorate appetisingly, I wonder why I ever resisted. A few pieces of fresh parsley clumped close to the black pudding and haggis on the grills looks great, and again, guests often eat the parsley at the end of the meal. The much-derided daaysies are actually the flower of the coriander, and we use many other herbs and their flowers to decorate a plate, the sage flower being one of the nicest. So with all due apologies to t' bluedie Tourist Board, I now delight in these additions, which please the eye and enhance the dish.

Such comments from 'the staff' (as Himself is known by myself – behind his back) as 'It's taken you longer to put that bits of rubbish on the plate than it took to cook the food!' are studiously ignored and I refuse to acknowledge his nods of approval when the final ensemble and I head for the dining room, thinking 'the nerve of the man'. You see, one of his self-appointed duties is to inspect the plates before they head for the table. The head chef approving a dish for one of the top restaurants has nothing on him.

Our huge variety of main-course breakfast dishes can meet with glazed expressions from the guests, followed by the dreaded phrase, 'I'll just have the cooked breakfast' (when they want to come across as a casual eater) or 'I'll have the full cooked break-fast' (when it's from my favourite diner, the robust eater).

They're not stupid, they're not foreign, they know by looking at even a few of the choices that no dish other than the smoked salmon is served raw for the main course! I can't snap back, 'It's all cooked,' now can I? Of course, I'm not stupid either – at least, so I keep telling myself, despite many who would cast doubt on that assertion – so I know perfectly well they mean bacon, eggs and anything that goes with them, though some screw up delicate noses at the offer of haggis or black pudding, while others cannot wait to try such Scottish fare.

Sourcing a local supply of ingredients gives ample opportunity for guests to find out more about the area they chose to stay in, keen now to shop locally, returning with supplies of the wonderful Golspie-milled oatmeal from our local Melvich stores to ensure they can still have a taste of Scotland long after they head for home.

Mind you, some say, 'Oh, I'll just have the full English.' The full English consists of Scottish bacon, eggs from as good a Scottish hen as ruffles a feather, sausages made by a butcher that can roll his 'r's with the best of them, black pudding and haggis made all of 17 miles away with fried bread that as often as not is made by my own fair Scottish hand – with Scottish flour. When possible those wonderful Scotch tomatoes are used, but then, to sully an all-Scottish plate, I have to admit the mushrooms may well have travelled from England, allowing authenticity to this sobriquet used as often by foreign travellers as our countrymen from south of Hadrian's Wall.

So one smiles and nods the head, and if in a teasing mood says, 'You're not going to try a Scottish breakfast then, seeing you're in Scotland?'

'What would that be?' you're sure to be asked. 'Porridge and kippers?' And some actually do take the opportunity to have locally-milled oatmeal, followed by a Loch Fyne kipper – not forgetting the bunch of thyme – locally-smoked haddock, or herring in oatmeal, all considered Scottish dishes – but who says which seas the haddock or the herring swam in, or that their daddy was actually spawned in Scottish waters? It can be rather presumptuous to lay national claim to any wild Atlantic fish dish.

'Is that Scottish salmon?' I'm asked somewhat suspiciously.

'Caught in Scottish waters, by a Scottish fisherman and smoked in a Scottish smokehouse. I guess we can say it's Scottish!' Guaranteed to be delicious, served with triangles of wafer-thin Melba toast, good Scottish butter and wedges of lemon, along with creamy scrambled eggs. Not like the scrambled eggs a friend and I once had in a top-drawer establishment; we filled a juice glass with the liquid from them! Lots of guests actually ask, 'May I have the smoked salmon without the eggs?', which is fine but heavy on the budget, as it sits on the large breakfast plate in splendid isolation, pleading to be released from its embarrassment by trebling the quantity – never forgetting its bit of green garnish, of course.

We have yet to garnish the porridge, or adulterate it in any way, pouring scorn on the winners of competitions who apply whisky, milk and all sorts of fancy additives to the cooking, then have the audacity to call it traditional. Guests are at liberty to add at the table: brown sugar – a firm favourite – Caithness honey, home-made jams and even maple syrup, or the more common milk. But the greatest favourite for the adventurous is rhubarb. The man Himself makes our highly-acclaimed porridge. It is worth noting that, before his old dog union allowed him to take over this early morning chore, my porridge was never highly acclaimed! He uses water and oatmeal, with one secret though quite authentic ingredient, winning him accolades for making the best porridge our guests ever tasted. The quality of the oatmeal is paramount, yet he preens each time I carry this praise back to the kitchen, where he keeps out of the guests' way and tells me I'm just jealous when I say, 'They probably tell that to all their hosts!'

Just this year a guest asked if we made the porridge with whisky. 'No!' said I, 'We make genuine traditional porridge and wouldn't dream of adding anything to it.'

'I don't want it then,' said he, nonplussed.

Couldn't have that, could I, so I suggested he place the order for porridge and trust me. Most people do trust you, when you have full control of their food and they have no idea how you produce it. I often wonder if this is why people you instinctively know are not naturally nice, are awfully nice to you. Maybe they think you just might adulterate their food, in revenge, if they let their natural angst take over.

'I don't want whisky in my porridge,' recoiled this gent's fishing companion, and two other guests who had already ordered porridge looked up in horror at such a prospect, while another's face lit up in hope as he enquired, 'Do you get many police out with the breathalysers of a morning in remote areas like this?'

Yes, we do actually, as some people know to their cost, having partied the night before heading for work, back before the media ensured we were all aware how long alcohol can actually stay in the system. I idly wondered how a judge would look at the indignant excuse, 'It has to be the whisky in the Sheiling porridge!'

They got their porridge as it should be next morning, and so did our fisherman, along with a large glass of malt to do with as he wished. And he did; he poured the whole lot on the porridge, stirred it up and got tucked in. Each time I entered the dining room, his colour was higher and his grin wider. He set off for the river in great feckle and declared it to be the best porridge he ever tasted. I'll bet it was! The hopeful man, meanwhile, was persuaded by his concerned wife to make do with the aroma drifting off the other's hot porridge.

Breakfasts have come such a long way since the early choice of take it or leave it, but there are still places you can stay where the owner looks at you with a heavy sigh and asks, 'Do you want the cooked breakfast?', proffering no menu and usually with one hand on hip, the other holding open the quick exit door, daring you to delay with unnecessary questions like, 'And what might that be?' You just know you'll make their day if you say, 'No, I won't bother with anything cooked.'

Could it be this attitude that gives rise to the quick, 'I'll have the cooked breakfast,' just in case there's any attempt to deprive you of the very service you are paying for?

In such accommodation, along with that appalling attitude there usually goes a mean glass of orange-coloured liquid, a thin slice of white toast with a tiny, pre-packaged butter and similar-type marmalade. Should you get the alternative, a grubby-looking slab of butter liberally sprinkled with toast crumbs exhibited on a communal dish, along with a sticky pot of marmalade with last week's spoon still in it, you would probably be grateful for the pre-packed varieties. Indeed, you do get some lovely tiny jars of good-quality preserves favoured by conscientious establishments who serve breakfast to lots of guests.

Individual little pots for butter are hygienic and economical but also labour-intensive. When I eventually sourced what I grew up to know as butter clappers, I found butter balls a highly attractive way of addressing both the hygiene and the cost factors. Prepared in a covered dish of iced water and kept in the fridge, they are ideal, except they take on a life of their own when released.

'Aaaahhhhhh!' Crossing the kitchen floor on way to dining room with full plate, my howl was often heard a mile away as I skidded on a butter ball – fish, poached eggs and nicely-arranged garnish, of course, sent flying. The economy is lost along with your composure as you quickly prepare another serving and try to remove greasy butter from the floor.

'I'm impressed with the variety of home-made preserves you set out,' my Scottish Tourist Board inspector began, but before I could glow in such praise he added in a very disparaging tone, 'but I cannot understand why you don't serve marmalade.'

'I do,' I replied, torn between indignation and hurt that he would think anything offered on the menu would be left off the table. Did the man not realise where he was? (In the early days my inspectors were always women, but in later years I invariably got a man.)

'Well, you didn't today,' he knowingly asserted.

'I served it today, same as I always do.' Indignation had won. 'There were two pots of marmalade on the table, and what's more, it is home-made, with proper Seville oranges,' I added with emphasis. Arguing with one of these fine fellows is tantamount to suicide if you hope to achieve a higher grading, so I refrained from adding, 'Put that in your pipe and smoke it – outside!' Smoking even then got the thumbs-down from establishments with a conscience.

I then had a very respectable (as in high marks – having read about the nail and the tooth and the equine displays, you're not about to swallow any other claims to respectability, are you?) four-star rating from the Scottish Tourist Board and had no ambitions to go further, although there is always a curiosity as to how the highly esteemed top rating could be achieved. I never believed that within a few short years the top accolade of five stars would be ours to have and to hold – the holding being even more difficult than the achieving, as many have found out after accepting the tantalising offer to be among the highest-rated in the country.

'In that case, I would like to taste your hand-made marmalade,' my inspector demanded, with such a glint in his eye that I knew he was convinced there was none. Of course I had hand-made – not even in this remote part of the Highlands would we use our feet!

Oh, the temptation to act abashed and give him the satisfaction of believing he had caught me in an act of blatant misrepresentation, and then pounce with my evidence. But inspectors have a difficult job without bored proprietors taking the mickey, so I escorted him to the kitchen, opened the fridge door and showed him the dish, then gave him a taste, and he admitted it was indeed home-made marmalade, and a very good one at that, and yes, that dish had been on the table, but he had not recognised it as containing marmalade. He had not lifted the lid.

But he was not finished yet. 'Why is it not in a pot marked "marmalade"? That would solve the problem,' he persisted, inspectors not being used to losing ground in a contretemps with a proprietor. There was no problem until he arrived. It was in a beautiful bone-china dish, matching the dishes that held the jams, the honey, the butter and the other accoutrements of the meal, and a rough, fat, orange pot with a green, leaf-shaped lid marked 'marmalade' was not about to grace my table. But, as I said, they have a hard job, so I just smiled the inscrutable smile we learn to adopt when the inspector calls. Now my guests breakfast on this story as I guide them through the various jams, pancakes etc. on the table, making sure they know that it is marmalade that hides beside the honey and the butter, not too far removed from the jams.

Nevertheless, I have reason not to wish a bad word said about this particular man. In a previous life he had been a chef, making him well suited to his inspection role with the Tourist Board – except of course, in this politically-correct climate, he and his colleagues are now called 'advisors'. My appreciation is for a very valuable piece of advice given during his visit.

He saw herring dressed in oatmeal served that morning. My method was to fry two filleted herrings and serve them with a garnish of dill or rosemary and a thick wedge of lemon. He suggested I take fresh gooseberries from the garden, make a piquant sauce, cut out the strip with the fin from the herring before rolling the four fillets in oatmeal, and serve, stacked attractively, with the sauce. He also hinted I call them goujons of herring on the breakfast menu. It is a fantastic dish and gets me plaudits he deserves, and this is an example of an advisor doing a great job. I can also add that this very same man is well respected in this area, an accolade seldom heard even a few years back.

14

One for the Pot

'PITY YOU DIDN'T have a salmon,' I said, 'and the river full of them just now.'

The line hissed and crackled. We had long graduated to owning a telephone; we even had a car at long last. Over the years we had seen a number of friends open their own B&Bs as the older women of the village slowly gave up the struggle to provide showers, separate lounges, hot and cold in the bedrooms, central heating and other facilities. The so-called discerning visitor, in particular the youth of what we knew as the Continent, wanted more than their parents had enjoyed, and the changes encouraged by the newly-emerging Quality and Standards Scheme saw a different product altogether being introduced to the market.

'Oh, yes. Well, to catch a salmon you first need a net, and I can assure you I don't have one.' That didn't surprise me. I knew Anne's husband would have a fit if any of the family, in particular his wife, took to helping themselves from the largesse of the river. What he did himself, as with most of the men who crofted, was quite another matter. Getting caught was to be avoided more in fear of what a landlord might decide to do about it rather than of the criminal proceedings.

'Bronco has one,' I said.

'I beg your pardon?' She sounded puzzled, so I explained that hidden away on her property, and wasn't that fortuitous, was the net Bronco had found, and carried, neatly stacked behind his saddle, all the way onto her croft, where my riding companion, who was a member of her family, had spirited it away.

'You did what? Do you mean to tell me that you and Sally have hidden a net in the tack room with all those riders tramping in and out?' She was not amused. I tried to change the subject, wishing I had kept my mouth shut. She wasn't listening. 'Anyway, it's probably some old cast-off, full of holes... do either of you realise the row there would be if that net was found by Steven? No, forget it. I'm in enough trouble as it is, taking that booking and offering them dinner at 10 o'clock at night. He'll go spare. I need that money though.' They lived in a fairly remote area and her having nothing suitable to cook for this unexpected arrival was understandable. Anne was a fantastic cook, generous to a fault, and had the requisite sense of humour to survive years of my friendship, but she was a lady who embraced risks with an enthusiasm that would leave you breathless. One thing was certain: a day or a night out in her company was never boring.

'The net's in excellent condition; not big, but big enough,' I assured her.

'So, you would know what to do with it then?' she queried.

'Well, not exactly, but I thought *you* would know,' I replied meaningfully. '*I've* never been out without a fully-qualified instructor.'

'You just keep your aspersions to yourself. I know no more than you do, but I'm desperate.' I could hear her brain calculating catching times, cooking times; but doing time would not have come into the equation. Poaching had always carried tremendous risks, and especially so now, with the growing tendency for a younger generation to put greed before need and not stop at one for the pot. The old-fashioned poachers frowned upon the gangs who cleared a pool to sell on all the catch. Poaching was beginning to get a bad name! The land owner made sure the river was seriously watched, their bailiffs far from popular in their efforts to do their job. Sneaking off with a net in the hours of darkness was a calculated risk, but going out on a pool in broad daylight was sheer madness. And in an area not too far from the road? Forget it.

'We're going to have to give it a try. And don't come back here just now with that horse. Take the car. I'm still trying to explain why he smashed up the gate.' Bronco and Troubie often lent a willing back with hacking and trekking, but Bronco was only ridden by my friend Sally as he could not be trusted like Troubie. The last time he had been out, he took extreme exception to being rested up after a hard morning hacking. He broke down a new wooden gate so he could join in a trek led by his stable-mate. I took him home in complete disgrace.

Keeping him out of the way seemed like a good idea so I got out our car, my pride and joy. I glanced at the teeth marks on the metal work; I had been intent upon dressing horses for a show and did not notice that Bronco was merrily munching on the brand-new car I had parked so safely on the other side of the fence.

'What on earth did that?' the mechanic asked, goggle-eyed.

'A horse,' I admitted, 'and if you can't do anything about it I will have no home to go to. And neither will the horse!' Without another word, off he went, and my heart soared in the belief this would be one equine trick I could camouflage. Back came my saviour, with several of his mates, all to look and laugh uproariously. They sent me off to the coach builder, who laughed even louder. His extortionate estimate was weighed against the effect the truth of the matter would have when Himself came home from the rigs. I left, anxiously clutching a small jar of what looked like similar paint to that on the car.

But being metallic, it was very difficult to match, and the incident was yet another black mark against Bronco, and me.

Anne and I rooted out the hidden net while I explained where we had found it. The horse had been crossing the river and refused to obey – nothing unusual in that – until he investigated something hidden on the bank. When we looked, we saw it was a net in an old jute bag. We left it there for days and no one took it. We didn't want it found by a water bailiff, so decided to spirit it away. Bronco was totally complicit, spooking about until we investigated his antics, and then happy to carry the spoils back to his lair.

Before long, Anne and I were on either side of a good pool and the net was set. Nothing happened. I shouted across, 'Listen, I think you have to encourage them into the net.'

'I'll have to get stones!' she called back. Ah ha! She did know more than she was admitting to, and with that she fired a reasonable-sized stone into the dark pool. It was a beautiful calm day and the loud plopping sound echoed in the hills like an explosion. With heart in mouth, we splashed more stones into the water and waited. The silence was heart-stopping. Suddenly the water erupted in volcanic upheaval, the noise stunning us.

A fish had hit the net, and it sounded as if all hell were let loose. Then a second one and an unbelievable third stormed into the net. The noise echoed through the valley as if to waken the dead. 'My god, you'll hear that racket a mile away,' we warned each other, wide-eyed with fright, furtively crouching, clinging on to the writhing net. 'Let's haul it in and get out of here.'

'We might get another one if we waited,' I suggested; the value of such a precious haul in dinners and delighted guests had me throwing caution to the winds.

'Are you mad?' my fellow felon snapped.

Probably, I thought, and began to haul in.

We had three large fish and getting the net in was no mean feat. At last we had it out of the water, into a jute sack, and we staggered off to an old outhouse, out of sight. Anne then produced a large stick and handed it to me.

'What's that for?' I asked as she unrolled each silvery beauty from the net, bending down to retrieve the third fish which was caught by the gills.

'To kill them with, of course.' Her voice was purely matter of fact.

I looked at her aghast. 'Kill them? *Kill* the fish? I can't do that. I can't *kill* them.' I was completely staggered by her suggestion, having thought of nothing past the thrill of catching them and converting them into smiling satisfaction round the table. The only fish I had ever caught had been landed on the opposite side of the river to where I sat as lookout. They were dead by the time I met up with them, the noise of the disturbed sea birds and the lap of the river, along with the thumping of my heart, smothering their violent transition from life to death.

'You've got to kill them, you fool,' she spat at me.

'I can't. Honestly.'

No way could I take part in such a massacre. I held back in misery as she ladled hefty whacks upon their innocent heads and with each effort gasped, 'No, you bitch,' Whack! Whack! 'you won't dirty your lily' Whack! 'white' Whack! 'hands, but by god' Whack! Whack! 'you'll eat them.' And so she chastised until all three lay dead on the floor.

At home the inevitable question was asked, 'Where did you get that fish?' The word salmon was seldom used, except when setting off legitimately to buy one from the fishing station at the mouth of the river, which one did now and again to ensure guests tasted the wonder of wild Atlantic salmon and to allay any suspicion as to how they came to taste it, should anyone care to ask.

'It was a gift.' True indeed.

'Where did it come from?' he demanded, surreptitiously looking around, for possession of a fish was a secret beyond sharing with anyone.

'From the sea,' I answered evasively.

'Aye, and by what means?'

'Swam, of course. They're good swimmers.'

I received such a warning of what a criminal record could do for my reputation that it was a long, long while before I found myself back on the river bank with a net in my hand.

Many a time, with funds low and guests to feed, what I would have given to chance it, but he would not take me on. He made the excuse that he had no suitable net, having lost his own expensive one in an episode that went wrong; fortunately it was the net that landed in the hands of authority and not himself. So of course I told him that if he did not have a net, Bronco did.

That was a mistake, for it was he, when an exciting fiancé, who had taught me the rudiments of poaching, an activity permeated with principles, closed mouths and honour among crofters who in no way believed themselves to be thieves. I was well lectured about the laws of give and take, and you did not take a net. Even if it was left hidden for weeks, you gave the owner every chance of picking it up, and if he didn't, you still left well alone. No mutterings of it being Bronco's find and he would not leave the bank without it did me an ounce of good.

Anne too was caught red-handed, though she got off with her one for the pot that night and her guests sat down to a delicious late dinner. Next day I called and she whispered to bring the car round to the door of the tack room and leave the boot open. We were to transport the third fish, as a gift, to a mutual friend. Both Anne's husband and her eldest son were at home and would thoroughly disapprove, so stealth was in order.

I almost got the car to the door but was blocked by the sudden appearance of husband on tractor. He left it there and headed for the byre. I dumped the car, opened the boot and hared off to warn Anne that it was not quite where she expected, but she was already on her way, carrying a sack in her arms close to her chest and going right past where husband and son had unexpectedly appeared. She rose to the occasion like a pro. 'Just giving Joan back her horse blankets,' she gaily informed them, while over her shoulder, her husband, son and I watched the large tail of a very fine salmon, flopping this way and that, slowly emerge from the sack.

Salmon began to slip off the menu as it became more and more dangerous to grab one for the pot. Of course we had the means to supply the table legally by buying salmon straight from the sea, and this was an occasional treat: grilled, baked, simmered, fried, even smoked, but never again poached!

High teas were traditionally served earlier in the evening than dinners, thus allowing for the suppers for which B&Bs in the Northern Highlands became renowned. Supper time had a great social atmosphere and was a fantastic opportunity for the guests to collar their hosts and get all their questions answered. Some hosts would sit in with them and debate pros and cons into the small hours. But eventually it was as much the suppers as the Tourist Board that rang the death knell for the high teas.

First you had to provide the tea, which was in effect a full main course accompanied by various breads, scones, pancakes, fancy cakes and shortbreads. This was fine, easily produced and served, even with a choice. But then, just as you had put away the baking, out it all came again to prepare the suppers, and ensure those who had not sat down to high tea would have enough to eat.

The first operators to ditch the traditional offer of an evening meal would often send their guests to the local hotel for dinner. This met with considerable annoyance from the management. A blustering indignant, 'They take the business that should be ours by right, then have the nerve to expect us to feed their guests!' was offered to all who would listen. It was only years later that hotels began to realise that the B&B proprietor was actually putting good business their way and that there was money to be made in encouraging B&B guests to eat in their restaurants.

Having to bring numerous social events to an early halt in order to get home to prepare guests' suppers became an intolerable burden for me. For instance, we were among the tiny group of founding members of the Melvich Gaelic Choir, along with two other B&B operators, and we all had to tear off early each session to get those suppers set out. This was so restrictive I reverted to my usual way of solving a problem that involved the guests: I discussed it with them.

We then relied heavily on word-of-mouth advertising and the army of return visitors who reappeared year in, year out. (Unless, of course, you were obnoxious to them, as some people actually were; the chickens came home to roost when the visitor chose to relocate and spill the beans round someone else's supper table. Not that you could always believe such tales, but if you were picking up someone else's business it usually meant the visitor had met with dissatisfaction.) The tendency to return repeatedly to an area, especially if the accommodation ticked all the boxes, allowed all the good B&Bs to build up a great trade.

My guests helped me devise a menu and eating time that suited everyone. I stuck to the grills that were the main course of the high teas but added many more vegetables to them and gave a very large choice, eventually reaching 13 different dishes. After this large course, which was brought about by buying in fresh from the fishmonger and butcher in Thurso, our nearest town, and individually freezing the main items, I offered a cheese board so opulent I could barely carry it. Copious pots of tea and coffee were served at the table, meaning there was no need to set up a separate table in the lounge. It was a reasonable buy for the guests and extremely popular, and it released me from the demanding suppers. Potatoes were served in a variety of ways but had to acceptably accompany each of the dishes on offer, as did the vegetables, which were changed on a nightly basis. The rest of the choice was up to the taste of the guest.

The cheese board and beverages allowed for a long stay round the communal table and with so many of the guests returning year after year, it was a convivial and fun time for all. For me, the meal was easy, in that after the main course was cleared you let them get on with it. Being inexpensive, everyone partook, so the ambience of the night continued in the morning, allowing breakfast to be a time of leisure and pleasure – just what a holiday should be.

This was a short interlude though, as tastes were getting more sophisticated and more people were sticking up signs, seeing B&B as an acceptable way of earning money. Prices were climbing and young people were realising that, with the help of development grants, they could enhance their homes to meet expectations. So, to retain our valuable trade and bring in new business, I began to concentrate on full dinners.

That's when the real fun started! Ambition, not just for myself but for the whole of the industry as I saw it, got a hold of me and I clung to it like Skooker with a bone. As I got the dinners underway and my reputation grew, I brought in new customers with higher demands. I would meet those demands. I would exceed those demands. Year-on-year I began to compete with myself over how I could reach the golden target of 100% occupancy. I had little interest in competing with others, only myself, and having started, I was dogged in my determination to reach all my goals. But two rules were kept, for the sake of my sanity.

The first rule was that our family, not forgetting the animals, required attention too, in particular our son, who was growing up encumbered by the needs of other people and having to learn to stake his own claims, which he did in a manner that sharpened his wits and kept me on my toes. He would gauge my activities and ask for the very thing he knew I would normally refuse just when I was cooking for us all, every sense focused on the job in hand. Oh, the fox!

'Can I go off fishing to the rocks?'

'What? What was that you said?' I flew round the pans, sorting and fixing and getting it right, eye on the clock.

'Fishing.'

What was this child talking about, I wondered as I concentrated on getting the main course all ready at the one time. 'Fishing? What about fishing?'

'It's a good night for it.'

'Yes... yes,' glancing out the window, 'it's a super night.' Obviously now a fraction of my attention was on the weather.

'I'm ready to go, then. That ok?'

'Go? Go out? Yes, of course, it's a fine night. I'll see you later.' He had eaten his dinner earlier. Later, I wondered where he was, and a dash outdoors to search about ended in a howl of terror as I spotted the tiny figure on the edge of the rocks with the tide fast approaching. It was a long way to the shore and he could so easily be cut off. Some instinct seemed to coincide with my fear as I watched the figure move towards safety; the temper was off me by the time he trudged up the land, fishing rod over his shoulder and fish swinging from his hand.

If it weren't fishing, it would be can Troubie and I go off to places I preferred we saddle up together to access. As he got older, it would be can I cycle off to unimaginable places, or can I go and play pool in the back room of the pub. When that one was put over me, he saw it as the ultimate in achievement, and having set the precedent, it was the most difficult to control. If I didn't concentrate better, I could add 'bad mother' to the growing list of 'qualities' I occasionally heard I possessed.

His tactics were honed over the years, and the homecoming was always expertly effected so that the row was avoided in the relief that he was safe. It is little wonder he joined the Marines and continued his shock tactics by phoning from the other side of the world, then popping up at the back window with no word of warning. He knew that my days flew by, allowing me to think he had spoken from Norway or Canada only the day before. My open-mouthed, wide-eyed shock made his day. Once, when I thought him in Norway, he telephoned from just along the coast. He had actually jumped ship, sped ashore, pleaded to use a lonely guesthouse telephone on the shores of Loch Erribol to phone 'Mum', then got back on board without discovery, delighted to have set foot on Scottish soil to 'surprise' his mother, who thought him safe aboard ship. Thank goodness there were no pubs nearby or he might have been clapped in irons, as I'm sure the lure of a quick game of pool would have won over his need to get back on the ship.

The second rule was that we would not turn our sitting room into a bedroom. We were derided time and time again for not converting this fine room to sleep guests, when Himself had spent an entire winter converting the loft into two bedrooms for our family, allowing us to use all three downstairs rooms for guests. Friends wondered with all the business being turned away why we did not make it four guest rooms by converting the sitting room too. But my first priority was getting hot and cold facilities in the bedrooms, and we still had only one bathroom, though we did have that magic shower installed. So, for a time, three guest rooms would have to be sufficient, though my active brain ensured nothing stood still.

The following article, the first I ever had printed in the press, gives an insight into how my dreams drove me on. This was written 17 years into my career, while cornered in the dining room surrounded by most of the contents of the kitchen, during our second big renovation of the premises. Snow gently fell on the fields and the horses raced around, excited by this change in the weather, tails high and feet flying. Felix, zat gridee cat, watched their display from the garden wall. The cat reminded me of our first big venture into shifting walls. The article was titled:

The Builders' Cat!

I once read a snippet which gave three golden rules to help retain sanity when the builders take over your home. First, make friends with the builders or put the second option into effect: if you have neither patience nor sense of humour, go on holiday! For me, patience is dependent upon the time and hassle it takes to get to the actual building stage, and my humour fluctuates according to how often is the electricity going to be off, or how long it takes to locate the missing cat. In our house, this is for the sake of the builder more than to prevent the cat from being holed up under the floor boards for the duration.

Our cat took to sneaking into the dark recesses of the loft to await the first unsuspecting plumber, chippy, sparky or husband who crawled along, instinctively knowing when to sensuously rub a furry body against that inevitable gap between jeans and sweat shirt. The resultant emergence of the victim painfully rubbing the top of his head and muttering fiendish threats became the prelude to locking up the cat in the greenhouse for the rest of the day.

Some women shift furniture to spice up the boredom of housewifery. I shift walls. It's much more exciting. When the light of my life built us a brand new home, I was happy with the walls, wherever he put them. The house was sufficiently large to do cartwheels of delight across the lounge floor and we could easily swing a cat in all of the bedrooms. Children were meant to fill those rooms, but after producing one fine specimen, being of a careless bent, I lost the recipe, and with trying being more fun than achieving, I was not inclined to mourn its loss. Instead, I filled those rooms with paying guests.

A number of years down the line, my expanding ambitions caused the walls to creep in on me, so after a long hard look at our surroundings and a longer sadder look at our bank balance, we got in the builders. This was the first time, a joint decision to which the cat agreed, subject to being ensured better sleeping quarters on completion of various extensions.

The builders duly arrived, for three long, arduous months, at the end of which I had many more walls, a cat in dire need of psychiatric treatment, and a squad of builders who left the premises a stone heavier than when they arrived. I was adhering to the first rule and got all I wanted done my way by exploiting their weakness for Black Forest gateaux, nicely poached salmon and lashings of tea.

Shortly after the builders left, I discovered my way was not authority's way. While complying with the frustrations of unnecessary red tape, I overlooked the essential Fire Prevention Act. The builders had to come back!

I was inspired to cope better with this prospect by taking a sudden liking to brandy. My better half coped by taking it out on me, and I took it out on the cat. The cat, who could not abide the merest whiff of brandy, did not cope but the now much larger house allowed all three of us the sanctuary of avoiding each other until we came to terms with the situation.

Back came the joiner and the electrician. I thought we were as well to have the bricklayer too, so conjured up a few jobs for him. Why leave out the gasman, hubby challenged, so into the middle of the chaos came the gasman and his team to give us fingertip control. The cat was heathenishly opposed to conversion and no longer amused herself with close encounters in the loft, now taking to howling her dissension into the wee small hours. It was her best ploy to date so that I too felt in need of a good psychiatrist.

It was as well the beleaguered cat knew nought of the Scottish Tourist Board who, in a bid to achieve anarchy amongst its members, shifted its goalposts, ruling that to retain present ratings, people who in their youth made do with an outside privy could now demand 'en suite' facilities.

So, back once again to the drawing board, and back came

the builders. I swore to the cat it would be a small job. Getting permission from the man of the house involved long negotiations, many measuring up confrontations – when I told him what I wanted and he told me what I would get, followed by candle-lit dinners in front of blazing peat fires to ensure I got what I wanted. The cat, being an ardent feminist, disapproved my methods but in due course, we were once more under the hammer, and the chisel, and the saw.

It was then I had the bright idea of enlarging the existing bathroom, seeing the builders were here anyway. My spouse's unconditional surrender – especially when he threw all caution to the winds and encouraged me to enlarge an upstairs shower room – should have warned me the deviousness of a man's mind.

That decision, and there was no turning back, necessitated a completely new staircase, which in turn involved the tearing apart of two bedrooms, the landing and the last remnants of my sanity. The smirk on my husband's face was definite proof he knew exactly what he was about when I vowed, never, ever again.

The work proceeded, albeit in a 'cart-before-the-horse' fashion due to lengthy wrangles with officialdom followed by a plea to the Highlands and Islands Development Board, before they metamorphosed into the Local Enterprise Company. In dealing with the HIDB I made the interesting discovery, Englishmen smile at you more often whilst saying 'No!' more emphatically and only a last minute tantrum bore a little of the fruit I had hoped for.

Things went exceedingly well until the plumber broke his foot. The fact I had broken my leg a few days before was not nearly so devastating. No other plumber could possibly wind his way round the intricacies of our system. It all ground to an ignominious halt and, with my leg in plaster, I soothed the outraged cat who sniffed the abandoned tools with feline disdain. I knew just how she felt.

Was it all a lesson to me? I'm afraid not. Being an optimist,

I revelled in the end product and forgot the trials, dreaming forbidden dreams, while stroking the unsuspecting cat. It took many a blazing peat fire followed by reverberating hammer blows to get the walls where I really wanted them.

The cat has mellowed and meets whatever onslaught with whimsical tolerance, closing her ears when I insist, this really will be the last time!

Oh, the third piece of advice for when the builders come. Never lose sight of your cat!

15

High Jinks and Hard Work

LONG BEFORE WE made structural changes, dinners became the order of the day, with mistakes made and lessons learned on the hoof. It was driven home on more than one occasion that you could never take for granted as the way forward any given situation that worked out satisfactorily – not until it was tried and tested several times.

For instance, when the new school in the village was built, two young heating engineers came to stay, just as I was keen to sort out menus and see how I would cope with proper dinners. Working men required a good solid meal at the end of the day, none of your high teas or grills, but a three-course meal. They were excellent guests. They saw little of the holiday makers as they breakfasted very early, but they came home in time for dinner, which proved no problem, and ate along with the other guests. We broke the second of our rules and gave up our sitting room, seldom having time to use it, turning it into a TV lounge for the guests, allowing peace for those who wanted to watch TV, while the other lounge with its fantastic view over the bay was shared by guests who preferred each other's company. Everyone was free to filter back and fore, watching news or whatever else, in a convivial manner.

The heating engineers were intrigued by Bendy, the only house rabbit they ever heard of, and the bold rabbit was delighted to sit with them of an evening. They proved far more interesting to him than 'ordinary' guests.

In those days a mail bus ran along our coastal road, delivering passengers and mail and all sorts of gossip and craic. I knew the driver, Hughie Reid, reasonably well. The bus drove to Thurso early in the morning and made the return journey through our village in the middle of the afternoon. One day I spotted Bendy sitting on the grass verge by the road, but before I could move from the window to fetch him back, he ambled onto the tarmac and sat upright, bang in the centre of the road, as if to stop and wash his face. My heart leapt into my mouth. What a spot to pick for ablutions!

We were all deeply attached to the rabbit by now and he was well known throughout the area as well as by our guests. The children of the village visited him, and to have him run over would have been unforgivable. He had a passion for chocolate and mandarins, which he would take in his front paws as he sat up on his hind legs, biting into the slivers, the juice running down his little black chin.

Seeing him on the road, I rushed off, prepared to run down the first field to rescue him. But by the time I got to the front door the mail bus had appeared and Bendy began a slow loping gait: a leap to the right, then to the left, then a few lopes up the middle of the road in front of the now crawling bus. I held back in horrified silence. What was he up to? When he reached our driveway he made a slow turn off the road and the bus drove on. He then sped back to the house.

I saw this performance several times and felt both puzzled and embarrassed. It was early spring and there was little traffic on the roads, and what traffic there was moved at a much slower pace than today's frightening blurs, but nevertheless it was a highly dangerous practice. My young engineers thought it wildly funny, so when they were about I would persuade them to go down and grab the rabbit off the road.

One day I looked out to see the bus had stopped. The driver was out and chasing Bendy up the road while interested passengers leered out the windows. Laughter could be clearly seen, if not heard above the engine, which had been left running. When this happened again, heart in mouth I ran down to apologise, for by now acquaintances had warned that the driver was thoroughly cheesed off with both the delay and the laughter of the passengers. He was a lovely man and said the rabbit never bothered him in the mornings, but his appearances in the afternoons were now becoming unacceptable! He was genuinely concerned that these antics, whatever instigated them, would cost the rabbit his life.

Many a debate we had on the whys and wherefores, the only acceptable answer being that he had become attracted to the vibrations, slow and ponderous as the bus wended its way up the slight incline towards his patch. A great effort was made to ensure he cut the habit.

It was not long after this that he became confined to the house when he contracted myxomatosis, and the months-long fight to try and save his life took up all the spare time I had.

By then our boys had completed their work at the school and left us with the impression that looking after working men was another good way of filling the bed spaces and making sure business continued to grow. That summer also left me believing all rabbits made fantastic house pets, and I could not understand that this was not universally accepted. They were clean, well behaved and highly intelligent, given the opportunity to develop. Boy, how wrong I was proven – on both counts.

Our son must have been about four when we gave him his lovely room in the loft conversion. It was a twin room so he could entertain his cousins and friends, and was loaded with a good selection of books and toys, with two large built-in wardrobes. By today's standards he kept the walls remarkably free from posters, though he loved his room.

By the time he reached seven his one ambition was to get a racing bicycle he could ride on the roads. I was not keen. He had a Raleigh in mind, and a determination that outwitted me.

'Can I get a bike?' I was concentrating hard, clearing away the first course and finishing off a sauce, so I prevaricated. 'A bike! What kind of bike?'

'A bike I can go to school on!' His replies became as evasive as mine, until I was just about to shoo him out of the kitchen. We lived a mile from the school, with the road getting busier each year. 'I'm smiling at you.' Since a very small child, whenever he thought there was a bit of trouble, be it of his or anyone else's making, he would put on a wide forced grin and say, 'I'm smiling at you.' I heard this statement made right up until he left home to make his way in the world and his charm offensive found other outlets.

Pressure for a bike went on for some time, until the day I was dashing about like a scalded cat, fridge and cooker demanding all my attention, when he came out with, 'If I save up all my pocket money would you match what I have so I can get a bike?'

'Definitely,' I assured him, grinning. He could never save money, didn't get that much pocket money anyway, and did not appear to be inclined to take on jobs at my going rate. To ensure I was on really safe territory I added, 'It is a Raleigh you want, and it is a new bike?'

'Yes,' he agreed, eyes shining, while I had a wee giggle to myself. Not a chance!

Not long afterwards, four chaps working in the area came to the door, looking for accommodation. They had heard the food was good here. So it was, but no way could I take them. I already had the two doubles occupied and only the twin left.

'They can have my room,' piped up the brat, who was well

used to answering doors, the guests enjoying his welcoming ways as he showed them round and chatted amicably, offering all sorts of hospitality. Obviously, he saw an opportunity to cash in on this manna his mother was keeping to herself.

'Don't be silly,' I said as I pushed him behind me, but the negotiator for the men had already pricked up his ears. Yes, they would take his room, he agreed. No way, I insisted. OK, could they have the available twin then? Yes, that would be no problem. They would book in on Monday.

For the entire weekend Neil bombarded me with every good reason why he should let out his bedroom and eventually I caved in. The agreement was that for each night he gave up his room, he would get a share of the profits. He soon had me hooked on how much more I could make if I had four rooms on the go, though he was holding out for 50 per cent. He worked like a beaver to prepare the room to the standards we insisted must be given to all who set foot over the door. They all paid the same rate; they would all get the same standards.

That's when the real fun started. I now had the little instigator of all my extra work sleeping in my room, when he wasn't whizzing about on his Raleigh. It worked out well enough as his father still spent weeks away from home. He was by now established in the oil industry as a rigger, working in both Orkney and Shetland. Whenever his dad came home, Neil was back in his own room and the number of guests reduced.

He began to spend a lot of time with the source of his new-found wealth, his enthusiasm knowing no bounds as he realised the extra money meant we could now afford to hire transport and event the horses in the three northern counties. We got Troubie from an excellent stable on the condition that this foal, who had won a major championship at his mother's foot, would continue to be shown as often as possible. Thus Neil and I retained our foothold in this world of excitement and great camaraderie. It was then that Sally, an expert horsewoman, came into my life and for more than two decades, horses were high on my agenda.

Despite having two lounges for the guests, travel-happy holidaymakers and working men just did not mix. At first, the men suffered from the over-attentions of the guests. Their idea of a good night was to relax in the TV lounge and glue themselves to the box. Guests were fascinated by the work undertaken in the area and quizzed them unmercifully. I could see their growing exasperation, but there were worse problems than that. The following extract from an old story tells why they had to go:

Eight people gathered in the lounge, working men all spruced up and ready to eat, guests lingering, asking questions and discussing their day. A glance could not distinguish visitors from the extremely presentable hydro boys, who worked on a scheme close by. They never put a foot out of place and never came to the table looking anything but immaculate.

Eventually all sat to eat.

I began to serve the soup; the two ladies first, then the men in indiscriminate order. I still had several to serve when one of the hydro lads leaned back and deposited his spoon in the empty plate, at the same time as one of the two couples presented me with a bottle of red wine to open. I goggled at the empty plates of two of the workers and avoided the eyes of those yet to be served, grabbing the wine.

I usually gave 10 to 15 minutes for the large plates of piping-hot soup to be supped, in a congenial manner, between much munching of melba toast, or delicate crumbling of rolls and idle adding of butter. Time was of no moment for my leisurely guests. Now there was wine to consider. Why had he not given this to me earlier, I wondered as I sped back to the kitchen.

I finished serving the soup, and began to pick up the by now three empty plates with a plan in mind. 'Would you like some more? You're most welcome.' That would keep them occupied while I dealt with the next course and set out wine glasses. 'Oh, no,' chorused my ravenous working lads. 'We're looking forward to the roast beef too much for that.' Foiled!

I dashed to the kitchen, where I had the most valuable help, which neither distracted, smiled at me, nor spoke back: a hostess cabinet. When used properly it was a godsend, allowing food to be kept perfectly while sauces and vegetables were finalised and guests were at their first course. Most items were ready and I blessed the hostess's perfectly-controlled heart, but I still had lots to do.

I cut thick slices of the huge roast – I hated those anaemic-looking thin slices floating in a sea of watery gravy that put profit before enjoyment. My mind honed in on what I was doing while my hands flew round the dishes, pots and pans, mentally debating every aspect of saving each second: Would I get some plates completely ready and start to serve? No! I would do as usual and get all the food plated before serving. Decisions, decisions! The sweat moistened my back as I worked with the hot Yorkshire pudding tray newly out of the oven, the sizzling roast potatoes, feverishly mashing creamed potatoes whilst buttering vegetables with my free hand. Why did I have to do so many different veg? There were times when I could shoot myself – often did, usually in the foot – but I would not learn, not when it meant cutting back or lowering a standard. I was going to do exactly the same thing tomorrow as far as the food was concerned, but I would have to put a better plan into action.

After completing the beef dishes, I added three plates of fish to the hostess and shot back to the dining room, remembering to compose myself before entering. I picked up only two empty plates. One member of each couple, swirling red wine leisurely round in the glass, was engrossed in quizzing the men, while their partners were animated in their interest in what was going on and ignoring their soups, which still had a few precious mouthfuls in the tip of the plate. I looked imploringly at my loquacious guests and the hydro boys looked imploringly at me. I fled.

In a lather of sweat, face red as my unfortunate choice of shirt, I dashed back to my stance by the hostess with the intention of serving the two guests whose plates I had lifted. No way was I going to give food to the lads first, so I concentrated on remembering were they 'fish' or were they 'meat'. Memories of a young waitress asking me whether I was a fish or a steak made me want to giggle, but this was serious work. I picked up the dishcloth and wiped my brow with it, until a voice from the wise old bird now sitting munching his own dinner shattered my concentration. 'I wouldn't do that if I were you,' came my son's stern rebuke.

'Well, you're not me, and you can be glad. And what's more,' I snapped as I balanced two plates, leaving the other hand free to field any obstacles, 'I'll wipe the floor with it if I want – or your lugs!' The cloth would be heading for the wash along with other casualties of the evening, but his fastidiousness at times exasperated me. He should have taken up residence in the shower room instead of plaguing me, the time he spent in there.

'Not the cloth. Harassing yourself like that. Make them wait.' He slowly shook his head in that familiar gesture of disbelief at my insistence everything was spot-on for the guests. This protectiveness was his only quarrel with strangers taking over his home. 'I'm smiling at you,' he assured me.

'Don't talk with your mouth full.'

He took off, announcing, 'I'm off to my other mother's.' That was not his name for his paternal grandmother, who lived up the road, but for Connie's mother, who treated him like one of her family; Connie's son was his best friend. He spent a great deal of time at their active smallholding, quite often sharing their dinner after he had demolished his own.

I had other things on my mind. I did not need to be told that the soup course had only served to whet the appetites of the working men. I saw the looks of anticipation, followed by hurt each time I entered and put down food in front of the others, urging them to make a start. Manners came second to my need to see them take up fork and knife before I dared serve the men. It was hard to take the beseeching looks of confusion as each watched, never taking their hungry young eyes from the four steaming plates set in front of their dining companions.

'Do start,' I brightly suggested again as I poured more wine, controlling the shake that began in my hands and was rapidly heading towards my knees. Was this the beginnings of heart failure? I just knew this job would be the death of me. 'It will take me a little time to serve everyone and I don't want your food to get cold.' I stopped in the kitchen to draw a long shaky breath and piled more beef onto their plates. Pity I couldn't have slipped a note to them saying, 'it will be worth waiting for'. But I deliberately popped the heaped plates into the hostess and drummed my fingers. The brat came back to pick up something or other.

'You got them done then,' he said as he eyed the roast, ready to grab a piece.

'Get your mitts off that. I've not served the boys yet.'

'I thought all the rush was to get them served before they died of starvation, and now you're standing there with nothing to do!'

'As if! Psychology, Neil, psychology,' I winked as I retrieved the plates and at last allowed the poor devils to eat.

Psychology or not, they were finished long before the others and I urged them to partake of the cheese board before their pudding, in the Continental style. But no, they would not have room, they assured me. Steamed syrup sponge with lemon sauce and fresh cream – they would not spoil that with the new experience of eating cheese between courses. Foiled again!

You know how today the term 'wilted' this and 'wilted' that has come to adorn menus? Well, in my day, the only thing in the kitchen that was wilted was myself!

Only main courses were pre-ordered, by guests who were

staying on, glad to study the menu in the morning; otherwise I had to be prepared to take the order right up to the last minute when arrivals were late. I took delight in offering three sweets each night, one always a hot pudding, the other two cold, sometimes with a cold sweet from the previous night, and each night I relished sampling them all myself. I was lucky that my energetic metabolism ensured I slipped into a size 10, as eating well was always high on my daily needs list, especially puddings. Had I not such a sweet tooth, there would have been an awful lot of waste. Puddings fuelled my energy!

'Will you get out of my kitchen and go to your other mother,' I demanded, slapping the hand that was helping itself to the beef. There was no time to bandy more words with him as I prepared the sweets and made the coffee and tea, swiftly setting up crockery in the lounge. By the time I cleared away I was absolutely shattered, more than ready for my puddings, worried about how I would cope for the duration of the hydro boys' stay. Never again, I decided – the needs of couples and families on holiday and those of working men are just too different to have a hope of keeping both groups satisfied at the same time.

This night had been the stuff of nightmares – something I discovered many who did bed and breakfast suffered from just before opening each season. In mine, I always tripped over the cat, hurling onto the floor the very last of the food in the house. I worried about this even before we had a cat, which should have been a warning never to get one, but warnings I was always poor at deciphering and heeding.

The man Himself said he didn't like cats, whereas I loved them. But then he and I were as different as chalk and cheese, he being a lark, me an owl; he viewing people with a need to know before committing and I always going for the hail-fellow-well-met approach.

We acquired Puss-Do when Neil was quite small. We had been encouraged to when I had rescued one of his friend's rabbits, another black Rex, from its hutch, offering to give it a bit of fun and games in the freedom of our large garden. I cradled it in my arms, wrapped in a scarf, as I walked home, past the house of a very kindly older woman who also did bed and breakfast and was generous in her interest in how I was getting on with my own new venture into her province.

She came out and enthused as she pulled back the scarf and saw the black fur, 'Oh, you've got a new kitten. Isn't it lovely. Children should always have pets and nothing better than a cat for a wee boy,' she nodded approvingly to Neil. Blackie's ears were flattened to his head and I don't know why I never made her any the wiser that it was a rabbit. Embarrassment, I suppose. But the little ears in the pushchair had cottoned on and before long we had our black and white cat.

We had her for only a couple of years. She disappeared – breaking a wee boy's heart – off the face of the earth before Bendy succumbed to his illness. Despite many searches we never found her and any talk of more cats was met with a rebuff from the man of the house. His home had never boasted a cat – a dog, yes, but not a cat – whereas cats were the only pets we were allowed as we grew up, and other than one black and white cat who made it clear she had time only for our father, I commandeered all others and grew deeply attached as they came in and out of our lives.

'Can I get a cat?' I was up to my eyes in clearing up, one eye on the clock, hoping to get the horses out on this beautiful summer evening.

'Look, your father says not. There's nothing I can do about that.'

'Everyone has a cat.' He was actually stacking the dishwasher, precariously, but helping at least, so I couldn't chuck him out.

'I know. I would love a cat. Over my dead body, your father said, and the last thing I did over his dead body, I'm beginning to regret.'

'He's away so much. We need a cat.'

'Like a hole in the head, I need a kitten to train at this moment.'

'Yes… a kitten would be much better. There's a cat who needs a home and we wondered if you would take it, but a kitten would be better.' He grinned. 'I'm smiling at you.'

'We're not getting a kitten. Now grab our hats and let's get going before that phone rings.'

We clip-clopped along the road, Bronco demanding lead role. The persistent hectoring continued from behind as I concentrated on controlling Bronco's usual exuberance. 'How old would a kitten need to be before we could get it?'

'We are not getting a kitten.'

'It would keep all the mice out of the house.'

'Will you heed what your animal is doing, Neil? Stop Troubie biting Bronco's bum,' I yelled as Bronco bunched up, head swinging backwards, the unexpected movement slipping the reins through my gloves. 'We don't have mice.'

'We do so!'

OK, so we did, but that was beside the point. 'All croft houses have mice. It's a status symbol.' We had sheep but didn't have a working dog. We had mice and didn't have a working cat. So what? Life would be very boring if we all had to conform to the same pattern.

'We don't need a collie dog and we don't need a working cat,' I offered.

'I never said anything about a dog. I would like a dog though. Can we have a dog then?'

Oh, hell! We were moving towards dangerous waters.

The pestering wasn't going to stop. By the time we brushed down the horses in the stable, with its aromatic feel-good cosy atmosphere, the deal was struck. If he could get his hands on a black kitten, it would be his. Easier than a dog, I assured myself, and he would never find the kitten I insisted we had to have. 'Remember, it has to be a tomcat. A boy cat would be lovely, an all black one, remember,' I enthused, even though I was certain he would find no such animal. Deal done. Peace at last. I doubted there was a single all-black cat in the entire village. I had always coveted a black tomcat or a red queen, types that had never come my way, but was well over my hankering now, believing any cat would merely add to my workload. I was convinced his quest for a black tom would meet with failure, for had such an animal spread its progeny in our village, I would have known. At that time we knew every household in the vicinity, our family being very much part of the social interaction of the area.

In a remarkably short time, or so it seemed to me whose life sped by on wings, the child announced he had sourced a black kitten. I quizzed him, but it was black, and a tom, and I had promised. I was sitting, one otherwise dull evening, on the deep freeze, a favourite perch, beside the table with the telephone, when in he came, with his friend Ellis, Connie's son, clutching a tiny black kitten. He held it with one hand under its chin, the other round its tummy. Ellis was grinning fit to burst. They were such small boys as I look back, recollecting every detail of the incident.

'It's your kitten.' Ellis proudly informed me. He loved cats and had several, encouraged by his granny, who insisted upon keeping a breeding queen, from whence had come the black kitten, along with most of the house cats settled in, by hook or by crook, to every household in the vicinity. The mother was tortoiseshell, small and beautiful, and this was her only black kitten ever, now eight weeks old. Boy, had I fallen for that one! The kitten had already been born when we made our bargain.

The little tom was gorgeous, I rapturously agreed, as I stroked his glossy fur and oohed and aahed over him, just as the boys knew I would. The phone rang. It was Himself! I looked at the kitten as I listened to the fellow who had put a 'dead body' ban on the introduction of any more cats into the household say he was at the airport – some unexpected time off – and would be here within the hour. Wasn't it good he gave us a warning, was all I could think.

'Right! The kitten is lovely and of course he is yours,' I said to Neil, ready to honour my promise, but to Ellis I urgently insisted, 'Take him back to his mother for just another week, to make sure he is ready to leave her.'

It took considerable guile to convince Himself the value of having a cat back on the premises, no mention being made until he was back at work and had to put his objections across a crackling line, weakening any case he tried to make. We all became very proud of our lovely black tomcat, despite the fact that on his second introduction to our home we sussed out the two tiny white patches, one under the chin, one on the belly, that my son and his friend had so surreptitiously hidden. But how could I send him back? 'I'm smiling at you' came into full play as I pointed out the few white hairs.

During Felix's first year we were given our second rabbit, a tiny bundle of black fur – a Silver Fox crossed with Black Rex – which our tomcat took to mothering. I had been conned by the white hairs but did not discover the second failure to meet the criteria until Felix went missing.

Neil was up in his own room and we were using a down-stairs room – the obligatory spring testing of facilities, possibly – about three days after his cat disappeared. The child was heartbroken, remembering the loss of Puss-Do. In the middle of the night, scurrying footsteps were heard racing down the stairs.

'I can hear Felix!' our son burst into the bedroom, wide awake, convincing us the cat was somewhere in the house.

Listening intently, we eventually heard the faint miaow. It took ages to trace it to the depth of the under-stairs cupboard, the one that eventually would store *that* bed. Bags of knitting wool, half completed garments and sewing stuff were all bundled at the back. We got a torch and shone it into the nether regions where the stair met the cupboard floor. Two large green eyes blinked back. The cat then shot past us, rushing towards the front door. Racing into the garden he briefly hunched under a bush before running back in, the widdle still dripping from him. It never twigged on us until he dived back into the depths of the cupboard what had happened. 'He' had been in kitten and there were 'his' three offspring, tucked out of sight. And what a job we had persuading our transformed tom to accept Skooker's old basket and behave like a normal nursing mother. Somehow she seemed to think she had to hide the kittens from us and it took time to entice her and her family into the body of the house.

We had the most tremendous fun with her kittens. All were eventually homed, but in the meantime our guests spent more time in the kitchen playing with the basket of fun than in their lounge and Felix delighted in the attention. She answered always to her name, never Pussy, so her misnomer stuck.

It was she who provided the morning entertainment for the guests. She hunted rabbit, as do most croft cats. She seldom took home her kills, other than the live mice she delighted in dropping at Barbara's feet, who did not appreciate the gift. But Felix did bring home tiny baby rabbits. From the warrens at the back, from down the land, from wherever she could, she took them home and, if not caught in the act, hid them away behind doors. Most we were able to return to the burrows but some had to be kept for a short while to restore their equilibrium, and this appeared to be her motive. She would nurse and play with them and thoroughly mother them while they were in the house. Sometimes she took them out from their hiding place herself, other times we knew by her excited, agitated gait that she had a rabbit stashed away, and the hunt began.

What amused the guests was the sight of their head cook and bottle washer, in the middle of serving breakfast, abandoning all to a full leggy flight down the field in order to waylay the cat and return a baby rabbit. The quicker you did this, the better. Once she brought back the same baby three times, a fluffy little bundle that seemed perfectly happy to be carted about, kitten style, by a cat. He had a tiny scratch on an ear which identified him. It was madness and took a bit of explaining.

'What *are* you doing?' when I puffed back into the dining room.

'Putting the rabbit back,' as I picked up plates.

'A rabbit? And to where?' queried the bemused guest.

'A baby. To its burrow.' It always took as much time to explain as to return the creature, so it proved a time-consuming exercise, but it sure kept me fit.

Felix became a great favourite with our regular visitors, stamping a gentle but very firm paw-print on the premises. She took exception to dogs, sussing out which cars held the canines and would sit on the wall, ready to stand guard at the gate, sometimes going so far as to refuse to let the dog out of the car. Yet, a dignified friendship developed between her and Mr MacTavish, a spirited Border Terrier who accompanied his delightful owners, Hugh and Kathleen Street, staying for a month as often as not, sometimes bringing his two cousins and their owners, which was pushing his luck a bit, but Felix forgave him and Christmas cards were exchanged with little informative notes until at 21 years of age, Felix made her final journey to the vet.

I was left with the task of breaking the bad news – though veered away from the black-edged cards – to those firm favourites, among them Denis Shrimpton who went so far as to bring a tape recording to take back home her loud satisfied purring when invited in to their lounge, as she always was, after dinner to keep company with the guests during coffee time. The moment she smelt the coffee she paraded the kitchen, ready to go. Peter Clark too, who joined us with his wife, Pat, all of 20 years ago, as did the Gunnyeons who also had to be told, their sons Kenneth and Malcolm having made a great friend of the cat. Sue and Steve Girbow too, whose son Lee introduced us to the joys of having a pet seagull for the next 20 years! The Clarks and the Gunnyeons were among the last of our long-standing guests to bid farewell to The Sheiling towards the end of the 2007 season, but even in that, we found laughter.

For that final visit, Bill and Joan Gunnyeon brought with them their sons and their partners, taking over the house for a nostalgic weekend when we went back to the old house-party atmosphere, hosting a dinner party on the Saturday night to the sound of popping Champagne corks and much merry laughter as the eight of us sat round the dining room table, reminiscing. When it came to saying goodbye on the Monday morning, I happened to have a meeting and had to go before their much more leisurely leave taking. It was they who stood in the doorway and waved me off, with Himself beside them, grinning all over his face, every inch the Landlord. And this was the man, all of 40 years ago, who threatened, 'Over my dead body!'

Conclusion

What Will Tomorrow Bring!

SO THERE YOU HAVE IT! I've taken you through some of the good and the bad of 40 years in the tourism industry. You're bound to think there's more to it than that and of course you're right, there's a great deal more.

The B&B industry has come a long way in the last 40 years, but many are now ready to say it has lost its identity, pointing the finger at 'standardisation', brought into effect by VisitScotland to ensure the visitor knew what to expect from the various star ratings. That was no bad thing, but as with all rules and regulations, operators look for sensible monitoring which allows individuality – within the confines of meeting expectations – to ensure B&B will always have its own special identity.

A cry heard often where more than two B&B people gather together is, 'They're trying to make everything look the same. Matching curtains and bedspreads are more important than the welcome!' Well, I once shadowed a Quality Advisor and walked into bedrooms that were a riot of clashing colours, an absolute shock to the system. Yet the Advisor said nothing about this during the visit, bringing up many other helpful points, in particular about IT knowledge in marketing, because that is what the operator was interested in.

Afterwards I queried the difficulty of being in such a disturbingly colourful room and was told that this was the operator's personal taste and they did not interfere with that, unless asked. Had there been a question about how to upgrade the establishment, then she would certainly have taken colour schemes into the overall picture. So, as ever, it's a case of listening to what each individual says and taking your opinion from what you're told, be it from the operator of a B&B or from VisitScotland staff. Personally, I believe B&Bs have more individual characteristics now than ever they had when I first started out in the industry. I remember there were hostels, hotels and B&Bs, with some self-catering. And that was it! Hostels were very basic, B&Bs had few facilities and hotels were for those who could afford them. Very few holiday homes were used for self-catering. But there were plenty visitors seeking accommodation, especially when we moved into the late '70s and '80s, though few booked up front and business tourism had yet to mushroom into what it is today. We had the occasional commercial traveller, but most stayed in hotels.

Things began to change, with B&Bs offering more and more facilities, and now you can search through the star ratings and book any standard you wish, offering as much comfort and choice as many top hotels. Prices, in comparison with the higher-rated hotels, remain extremely competitive; and at the other end of the market you can find a good, clean B&B with basic amenities to suit the lightest of pockets.

There are also a variety of B&Bs to serve different needs. For example, this growing tendency to kit out self-contained (not self-catering) accommodation in an area of the garden. This will suit many different travellers, such as those with dogs, new brides and old lovers seeking privacy, families with boisterous children – people who prefer the independence of their own threshold, yet enjoy the welcoming service of a B&B.

Yet nowhere can be more welcoming than a traditional,

well-run B&B – though at present there is little doubt the real growth market is in bona fide self-catering, considered to be every bit as viable but not near so much hard work as B&B.

Long ago, you never heard anyone come in to a hotel and ask at the reception desk for bed and breakfast. Instead, it was 'a room for the night', which automatically included breakfast, along with a table available at dinner. Today, you ring up hotels and have to ask for bed and breakfast, and if you don't book dinner, don't take it for granted that a place will be found for you, resident or not! Even hostels take bookings for bed and breakfast, as do bunk house accommodation, campus accommodation, restaurants with rooms, boutique hotels, inns, lodges, town houses and don't forget about trains, as well as the wifie down the road who doesn't need a sign put out because her sister-in-law passes on her surplus! Booking bed and breakfast has become the norm across much of the world.

It is, as they say, a different ball game now. So what will B&B's future be? Now there's a question many believed they would never need to ask, so sturdy was its growth until now.

We still see growth in the higher end of the market, where retired couples run rooms with excellent facilities, as and when they feel like it, to bolster a lifestyle that appeals to them. But we need much more than this to keep the balance of the sector healthy.

Modern families tend to make use of every room in their home, children having a bedroom each, enjoying their electronic games, spreading into any extra living space that could, in the past, have been used for B&B. Mums go out to work and see no attraction in staying home to devote time, money and effort to the comfort of strangers, despite the much higher income they could now expect from a B&B business, compared with a number of years ago.

I felt sure traditional B&Bs would slowly decrease in number for various reasons but nobody would have it. Now it is happening. Proprietors who have retired find few who will take their place. And would you blame them? Legislation is eating its way into even the smallest of establishments, demanding changes that will hurt.

Quite a number of B&Bs have provided an extra facility for their visitors, enhancing the social aspect of their stay; a provision that puts little profit into the accounts but allows guests the pleasure of buying each other a drink over a get together in the evenings: a table licence. Some hard-working people entice their guests to take their evening meal on the premises with the lure of that licence. Will they be able to afford the upkeep dictated by the new licensing law that came into effect at the end of November 2005? They say not.

Just a short while ago, the Performing Rights Society was phoning accommodations, including small B&Bs, asking if they had a radio or TV on their premises or in guest rooms. If the answer was yes, they demanded the owners pay a licence fee or face court proceedings.

Then there's the new fire prevention rules, with some very small B&Bs being sent out Fire Risk Assessment forms that assure them, regardless of their private status, they will have to pay for what is effectively commercial protection. The necessary renovations will cost much more than the profit they can expect for the next few years.

There is the ever-present problem in the catering industry of finding suitable staff, and this too can affect the future of B&Bs. Not everyone can lay their hands on a Barbara, Diane or Connie. Connie would have made the most marvellous tutor, preparing students to come into our sector. But B&B is not at the top of agendas when training in the hospitality industry is set up, though the skills now required are the same as for any well-run hotel.

I believe the B&B sector on the whole will survive, but not as it used to be. Most proprietors want to comply with sensible rulings that protect the visitor, but some of the legislation coming out of the European Union has little understanding of the running of small B&Bs.

One regulation tells us that family pets will no longer be tolerated in the kitchen. Listening to a debate on the car radio after a difficult meeting, my mood was lifted when I heard a B&B operator say, 'So, Rover can no longer doze by the Aga, then!'

'Listen,' came the quick response from the presenter. 'Some of the B&Bs I've stayed in, Rover would have made a better job of the cooking!'

I hope she never ever stayed at The Sheiling!

Recipes to Ponder from the Kitchen of The Sheiling

Creamy Scrambled Eggs

Take two large Eggs from the warm nest of a free-range hen and beat with a smidgen of Satisfaction.

Into this pour two tablespoons of Double Cream with a measure of Regret from days gone by when cream did not come in plastic containers but from a thick layer skimmed off a basin on the dairy-room shelf.

Put a chunk of Butter along with an ounce of Prayer for your guest's cholesterol into a warm pan.

Add a pinch of Common-sense Salt and a smile of Pepper into the egg mixture and toss into the warmed butter. Stir with a little Caution.

Serve sprinkled with a modicum of Modesty garnished with a measure of Sage.

Himself's Own Porridge

Take yourself out of the picture and watch as a careful handful of locally-milled Oatmeal is reverently lowered into an unknown quantity of Cold Water.

Observe a heartfelt sigh of Sea Salt added to the mixture,

soaked overnight with Patience until the morning brings a large number of Stirrings, sprinkled with some Declarations of Independence.

Watch as the mixture is cooked slowly with lots of Pride. Serve the laden plate along with some Innocent Smiles and a little of the chef's Wow Factor.

Bring back to the kitchen a Compliment of Praise and watch quietly as the chef burnishes his inflated ego along with the porridge pan none other must touch.

Fresh Haddock with Poached Eggs

Take a Lightly Smoked Fresh Haddock with a Prayer for those who provide the bounty of the seas and coat the fillet with Melted Butter.

Cook with Alacrity in a little Milk whilst watching a pan of Salted Water come to the boil and stir with Vigour. Into this drop two Eggs with Essence of Strong Confidence.

Place the eggs beside the fish and serve with Tomato Garnished Pride, but beware, too much Pride can spoil any dish – with the exception of Himself's porridge which can stand any amount of Pride.

The Full Scottish Breakfast

Take a Hungry Guest and place at table with the offer of a Plate of Porridge served with a good handful of Patience when the Full Scottish Breakfast is ordered.

Into the kitchen bring the side of a happy locally-bred Pig, smoked and sliced thinly, and place two slices under the grill. Turn frequently before guests are alerted to the goings on in the kitchen by the alarming calls of the smoke detector.

Take from the fridge two slices of Black Pudding, made

from the blood of the butchered pig, and place beside them a thick slice of Heather-fed Haggis, caught and hung 10 days before skinning and fry with two handfuls of Ability and a little of your big store of Patience.

Prick two Sausages made from the flesh of the pig and spiced with Abandon, pan-fry with a measure of Caution and cook through ensuring a glossy and well-done finish.

Cook Wild Mushrooms gathered from a nearby wood, slice, and fry in butter with a sprinkling of Hope and if Doubt begins to taint the mixture, add a good handful of Prayers.

Put Peppercorn and Cardamom Seeds into a pestle and grind with a measure of Impatience then sprinkle on peeled Scotch Tomatoes and grill.

Fry two Eggs in a light oil and serve with the other ingredients along with lots of Pleasure, on the largest platter you can find, with plenty of the Sauce of Satisfaction.

Notes

The Automobile Association

Since 1932 the AA has provided a vast range of services to the travelling public, including the inspection of accommodations and restaurants within its membership. Few small B&Bs joined in the earlier days, but its introduction of Diamonds when the Scottish Tourist Board did its ratings in Crowns proved an attractive marketing tool and many B&Bs signed up. Today the AA and RAC, along with all British tourist boards, use a standardised rating of Stars so as to simplify the delivery of quality standards for all visitors. www.theaa.com.

Board of Agriculture

Responsibility for all agricultural matters in Scotland, except for animal health, was transferred in 1911 to the newly-created Board of Agriculture for Scotland. Since 2001 the board has been known as Defra, the Department for Environment, Food and Rural Affairs.

Crofters Commission

This organisation is responsible for the development and regulation of crofting. Over 17,700 crofts, covering 25 per cent of the agricultural land in the Highlands and Islands, come under the tenure of this government body, which acts in the best interest of the crofters who tenant the croft land, most of which is owned by big land owners.

Green Tourism Business Scheme

VisitScotland introduced the GTBS Scheme in 1998 to encourage tourism businesses to be environmentally friendly. It gives bronze, silver and gold awards; useful marketing tools that, when run conscientiously, should allow for good savings that do not detract from a high standard of service. Join at www.green-business.co.uk.

Highlands & Islands Development Board

This was the public body responsible for delivering government grants to assist economic and cultural development. It was formed in 1965 and replaced by Highlands and Islands Enterprise in 1991. HIE's aim is to enable people living in the Highlands and Islands to realise their full potential on a long-term sustainable basis. As with the HIDB, much of the HIE's work involves the tourism sector and its sustainable growth.

Melvich Gaelic Choir

This choir has risen to great achievements over the years, considering its inauspicious beginnings. It continues to entertain many visitors with its undeniable talent, winning trophy after trophy in the Scottish National Mod.

The Prince's Initiative

North Highland Tourism is part of an initiative launched by the Duke of Rothesay (as HRH the Prince of Wales is known in Scotland) in order to highlight and market the tourism opportunities in the three northern counties of Caithness, Sutherland and Ross-shire. www.northhighlandsscotland.co.uk is well worth a visit.

Quality Assurance Scheme

This is a set standard laid down by VisitScotland. Each criterion is relative to individual Star gradings, documented in VisitScotland's package on how to achieve and maintain your standards. This can be found on their website www.visitscotland.org.

Scotland's Best B&Bs

A group of no more than 96 operators with four- and five-star VisitScotland gradings who take no more than six guests, run very successfully by a committee drawn from within the membership. Members are geographically spread throughout Scotland. There is usually a waiting list to gain entry into this very worthy marketing group. www.scotlandsbest.co.uk.

Scottish Tourist Board

The Scottish Tourist Board (STB) came into effect in 1969 under the Development of Tourism Act. Not until 1984 did the Tourism Oversees Promotion (Scotland) Act provide authority for the board to market Scotland overseas. In 2001 the STB began trading as VisitScotland.

Table Licence

Anyone interested in applying for a Table Licence would do well to check out current costs since the Licensing (Scotland) Act 2005 has come into effect. The Policy Statement of individual local authorities who have both the authority and the autonomy to oversee the Act in each individual area should also be scrutinised.

Taste of Scotland

The Taste of Scotland Ltd Scheme was set up by the Scottish Tourist Board in 1980 and gave a prestigious edge to food outlets who were invited to join, the marketing advantage being that you should not be able to buy your way into the scheme. There were for example 423 elite members in 2000, before it went into receivership in 2003. Today VisitScotland runs a similar-style food scheme, EatScotland, www.eatscotland.com, so the profile of Scottish food continues to be raised and visitors can still be pointed in the right direction.

Tourist Information Offices

These offices were set up in strategic communities, hosted by employees of the newly-emerging Scottish Tourist Board, there to serve visitors seeking information on an area. Their major job, until the advent of mobile phones rendered this particular service obsolete, was to book visitors into various establishments for the duration of their stay, initially doing so free of charge to either establishment or visitor. Eventually a percentage charge, paid for by the establishment, was introduced, with a small standing charge made to the purchaser of the accommodation. This booking service is now carried out through www.visitscotland.com.

Scotland Recommends: The word-of-mouth guide to Scotland

Edited by David Lee
ISBN 1 906307 47 4 PBK £7.99

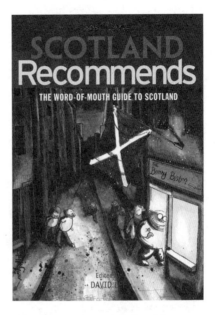

Have you ever stood in a strange street and wondered where to eat?

Ever queued for hours to get into a visitor attraction that turned out to be mince?

Have you ever wished you could speak to someone who really knew what to see?

Scotland Recommends is the savvy local you've been looking for. For over a year, readers have been writing in to the *Recommends* section of *The Scotsman*, telling the paper that they know a great little Mexican down Victoria Street or a spine-tingling cave in Ardnamurchan. These are the best (and most useful) of the home-grown endorsements, brought together into something better than a guidebook – it's more like a little friend to carry around in your pocket.

With a great line-up covering the basics (dog-friendly hotels, romantic restaurants, cheap places to eat), as well as the weirder holiday pastimes (wishing wells and trees, where to find conkers, the best public toilets) and the things that are just plain fun (traditional music venues, chocolatiers, places to build sandcastles), this book is designed to be useful for the native Scot as well as the holidaymaker.

Whether you're in Scotland for a day, a weekend, a week, or have been here all your life, this is the book for you. *Scotland Recommends* is the ultimate guide to having a brilliant time in Scotland.

Recommends *is a great supplement – even more fun than a bed bath in a private hospital.*
DOMINIK DIAMOND,
TV and radio presenter

The Northern Highlands: The Empty Lands

Tom Atkinson

ISBN 1 842820 8 77 PBK £6.99

 The Empty Lands are that great area of northern Scotland between Ullapool and Cape Wrath, and between Bonar Bridge and John O' Groats.

It is truly the Land of the Mountain and the Flood, where land and sea mingle in unsurpassed glory.

From the pier-head at Ullapool to the Smoo Caves at Durness, and from Dornoch Cathedral to Dounreay Nuclear Establishment, Tom Atkinson describes it all, with his usual deep love for the land and its people. Myths and legends, history, poetry, and a keen eye for the landscape and all its creatures make this book an essential companion for all who travel to that magnificent part of Scotland.

The essence of Scotland's far north and west is emptiness. Emptiness of people, that is, but of nothing else that brings delight to any tired soul, writes Atkinson, I have tried to convey something of the sheer magic of the Highlands, something of the joy that comes from such a cornucopia of loveliness, for the Highlands are lovely beyond words.

Scots We Ken

Julie Davidson

ISBN 1 906307 00 8 HBK £9.99

 'We dinny do bairns in this pub. We dinny do food, apart from peanuts and crisps, or music or fruit machines or video games. We jist aboot do television, but thon set on the wall is 20 years old and it only gets turned on fur internationals or Scotsport. This pub is fur drinkin.'
From 'The Last Publican'

Natives know them. Visitors soon get to know them.

Some, like the Golf Club Captain, the Last Publican and the Nippy Sweetie, are an endangered species; others, like the Whisky Bore and the Munrobagger, are enduring figures on the Scottish landscape. Every generation produces its own variations on the Scottish character and it doesn't take long for the newcomers to become familiar social types like the MSP, the Yooni Yah, the Country Commuter and the Celebrity Chieftain.

Most Scots, if they're honest, will recognise a little bit of themselves in one or other of these mischievous and frighteningly accurate portraits.

A triumph of canny Scots-watching.
MURRAY GRIGOR

Riddoch on the Outer Hebrides

Lesley Riddoch

ISBN 1 906307 86 5 PBK £12.99

Riddoch on the Outer Hebrides is a thought-provoking commentary based on broadcaster Lesley Riddoch's cycle journey through a beautiful island chain facing seismic cultural and economic change. Her experience is described in a typically affectionate but hard-hitting style; with humour, anecdote and a growing sympathy for islanders tired of living at the margins but wary of closer contact with mainland Scotland.

Let's be proud of standing on the outer edge of a crazy mainstream world – when the centre collapses, the periphery becomes central.
ALISTAIR MCINTOSH

She has a way of shining the magnifying glass on a well-documented place in a new and exciting way matching every beauty with a cultural wart that builds to create one of the most unfalteringly real images of the islands – all the more astounding for coming from an outsider.
STORNOWAY GAZETTE

Women of the Highlands

Katharine Stewart

ISBN 1 905222 74 2 HBK £14.99

The Highlands of Scotland are an evocative and mysterious land, cut off from the rest of Scotland by mountains and developing as a separate country for hundreds of years. Epitomising the 'sublime' in philosophical thought of the eighteenth century, the Highlands have been a source of inspiration for poets and writers of all descriptions.

Katharine Stewart takes us to the heart of the Highlands with this history of the women who shaped this land. From the women of the shielings to the Duchess of Gordon, from bards to conservationists, authors to folk-singers, *Women of the Highlands* examines how the culture of the Highlands was created and passed down through the centuries, and what is being done to preserve it today.

Details of these and other books published by Luath Press can be found at:
www.luath.co.uk

Luath Press Limited
committed to publishing well written books worth reading

LUATH PRESS takes its name from Robert Burns, whose little collie Luath (*Gael.*, swift or nimble) tripped up Jean Armour at a wedding and gave him the chance to speak to the woman who was to be his wife and the abiding love of his life. Burns called one of 'The Twa Dogs' Luath after Cuchullin's hunting dog in Ossian's *Fingal*. Luath Press was established in 1981 in the heart of Burns country, and is now based a few steps up the road from Burns' first lodgings on Edinburgh's Royal Mile.

Luath offers you distinctive writing with a hint of unexpected pleasures.

Most bookshops in the UK, the US, Canada, Australia, New Zealand and parts of Europe either carry our books in stock or can order them for you. To order direct from us, please send a £sterling cheque, postal order, international money order or your credit card details (number, address of cardholder and expiry date) to us at the address below. Please add post and packing as follows: UK – £1.00 per delivery address; overseas surface mail – £2.50 per delivery address; overseas airmail – £3.50 for the first book to each delivery address, plus £1.00 for each additional book by airmail to the same address. If your order is a gift, we will happily enclose your card or message at no extra charge.

Luath Press Limited
543/2 Castlehill
The Royal Mile
Edinburgh EH1 2ND
Scotland
Telephone: 0131 225 4326 (24 hours)
Fax: 0131 225 4324
email: sales@luath.co.uk
Website: www.luath.co.uk